instant manager
taking control of work and life

inspiring leaders

bookkeeping and
ACCOUNTING

ROGER MASON

HODDER
EDUCATION
PART OF HACHETTE LIVRE UK

Orders: Please contact Bookpoint Ltd, 130 Milton Park, Abingdon, Oxon OX14 4SB. Telephone: (44) 01235 827720, Fax: (44) 01235 400454. Lines are open from 9.00 to 5.00, Monday to Saturday, with a 24-hour message answering service. You can also order through our website www.hoddereducation.co.uk.

British Library Cataloguing in Publication Data
A catalogue record for this title is available from the British Library.

ISBN: 978 0340 972 861

First published   2008
Impression number   10 9 8 7 6 5 4 3
Year   2012 2011 2010 2009

Copyright © 2008 Roger Mason

Cover image © F Schussier/Photolink/Getty
Photographer (logo) Niki Sianni

Typeset by Transet Limited, Coventry, England.
Printed in Great Britain for Hodder Education, part of Hachette Livre UK, 338 Euston Road, London NW1 3BH by CPI Cox and Wyman, Reading, Berkshire, RG1 8EX.

Hachette Livre UK's policy is to use papers that are natural, renewable and recyclable products and made from wood grown in sustainable forests. The logging and manufacturing processes are expected to conform to the environmental regulations of the country of origin.

The Chartered Management Institute

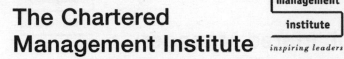

The Chartered Management Institute is the only chartered professional body that is dedicated to management and leadership. We are committed to raising the performance of business by championing management.

We represent 71,000 individual managers and have 450 corporate members. Within the Institute there are also a number of distinct specialisms, including the Institute of Business Consulting and Women in Management Network.

We exist to help managers tackle the management challenges they face on a daily basis by raising the standard of management in the UK. We are here to help individuals become better managers and companies develop better managers.

We do this through a wide range of products and services, from practical management checklists to tailored training and qualifications. We produce research on the latest 'hot' management issues, provide a vast array of useful information through our online management information centre, as well as offering consultancy services and career information.

You can access these resources 'off the shelf' or we can provide solutions just for you. Our range of products and services is designed to ensure companies and managers develop their potential and excel. Whether you are at the start of your career or a proven performer in the boardroom, we have something for you.

We engage policy makers and opinion formers and, as the leading authority on management, we are regularly consulted on a range of management issues. Through our in-depth research and regular policy surveys of members, we have a deep understanding of the latest management trends.

For more information visit our website **www.managers.org.uk** or call us on **01536 207307**.

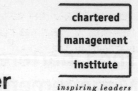

chartered
management
institute

inspiring leaders

Chartered Manager

Transform the way you work

The Chartered Management Institute's Chartered Manager award is the ultimate accolade for practising professional managers. Designed to transform the way you think about your work and how you add value to your organisation, it is based on demonstrating measurable impact.

This unique award proves your ability to make a real difference in the workplace.

Chartered Manager focuses on the six vital business skills of:

- Leading people
- Managing change
- Meeting customer needs
- Managing information and knowledge
- Managing activities and resources
- Managing yourself

Transform your organisation

There is a clear and well-established link between good management and improved organisational performance. Recognising this, the Chartered Manager scheme requires individuals to demonstrate how they are applying their leadership and change management skills to make significant impact within their organisation.

Transform your career

Whatever career stage a manager is at Chartered Manager will set them apart. Chartered Manager has proven to be a stimulus to career progression, either via recognition by their current employer or through the motivation to move on to more challenging roles with new employers.

But don't take just our word for it ...

Chartered Manager has transformed the careers and organisations of managers in all sectors.

- *'Being a Chartered Manager was one of the main contributing factors which led to my recent promotion.'*
  Lloyd Ross, Programme Delivery Manager, British Nuclear Fuels

- *'I am quite sure that a part of the reason for my success in achieving my appointment was due to my Chartered Manager award which provided excellent, independent evidence that I was a high quality manager.'*
  Donaree Marshall, Head of Programme Management Office, Water Service, Belfast

- *'The whole process has been very positive, giving me confidence in my strengths as a manager but also helping me to identify the areas of my skills that I want to develop. I am delighted and proud to have the accolade of Chartered Manager.'*
  Allen Hudson, School Support Services Manager, Dudley Metropolitan County Council

- *'As we are in a time of profound change, I believe that I have, as a result of my change management skills, been able to provide leadership to my staff. Indeed, I took over three teams and carefully built an integrated team, which is beginning to perform really well. I believe that the process I went through to gain Chartered Manager status assisted me in achieving this and consequently was of considerable benefit to my organisation.'*
  George Smart, SPO and D/Head of Resettlement, HM Prison Swaleside

To find out more or to request further information please visit our website **www.managers.org.uk/cmgr** or call us on **01536 207429.**

Contents

CHAPTER 06

WHAT PREPARATIONS ARE NECESSARY FOR PRODUCING THE ACCOUNTS?

CHAPTER 07

CHAPTER 08

CHAPTER 09

CHAPTER 10

Preface

Millions of sets of accounting records are maintained in Britain and countless others around the world. They range from the books of major companies with figures measured in billions, down to the cash book of a group of friends who have formed a club to pursue a hobby.

An understanding of the principles of bookkeeping and accounting is important for managers, and perhaps others too. It will help all managers, not just those involved in bookkeeping and accounting. Hodder Education and the Chartered Management Institute have asked me to write this book for managers wishing to master the principles and perhaps progress further.

Bookkeeping and accounting has the reputation of being rather a dry subject, perhaps suitable for stamp collectors and train spotters. I can understand this belief, even though as an accountant who likes both stamps and trains I have always found it fascinating. With this perception in mind I have tried to make the book as interesting as possible, consistent with fulfilling the task of properly explaining the subject. It is for you to judge whether or not I have succeeded.

Whether or not you like the book I am confident that you will like Chapter 5. This has been written by my friend and colleague Peter Hughes ACA. Peter draws on his experience with P. D. Hughes Consultancy Services and I am grateful for his important contribution. I am also grateful to my son, David Mason ACA, who reviewed the finished text.

Chapter 9 examines published accounts and you may find it helpful to have to hand a company's annual reports and accounts. A company that you know, such as your employer, would be particularly useful. It would help with Chapter 10 as well.

The book deals mainly with bookkeeping and accounting principles, which have universal application, but there is just a bit of law. With regrets for my (hoped for) overseas readers, it is of course British law.

Each chapter ends with some questions, so that you can test your knowledge of that chapter. **The answers are given at the end of the book, starting on page 187.** Many of the questions only call for a short answer, but some are detailed exercises that will take quite a bit of time. What you do with the questions is your choice. You might decide to ignore them, to do just some or to conscientiously do all of them. You could of course read through the questions and answers, treating them as extensions of the chapters. No doubt you will make the decision that is right for you.

Thank you for choosing this book. I have enjoyed writing it and I hope that you enjoy reading it, or at the very least find it useful.

Roger Mason

What are the basic principles of bookkeeping?

In order to understand accounting it is necessary to understand bookkeeping, and in order to understand bookkeeping it is necessary to understand the basics. This chapter explains the basic principles, starting at the absolute beginning. The topics covered are:

- What is bookkeeping?
- The importance of bookkeeping.
- Single entry bookkeeping.
- The concept of double entry bookkeeping.
- Three basic rules of double entry bookkeeping.
- Two examples of double entry bookkeeping postings.

What is bookkeeping?

This is a very basic but very important question, and it deserves a very basic but important answer. The following is taken from the first page of the first chapter of *Bookkeeping* by Andrew Lymer and Andrew Piper in the *Teach Yourself Series* published by Hodder Education.

What is bookkeeping?

The process of correctly recording in Books of Account cash, credit and other transactions.

What are Books of Account?

The primary Book of Account is called the ledger, so called because all transactions, after first being recorded in subsidiary books, are afterwards grouped or summarised in accounts in the ledger.

Why should goods or services be bought or sold on 'credit'?

Almost all business dealings are conducted on a credit basis to avoid the inconvenience and danger of carrying large amounts of cash. The supplier of goods or services is usually content to accept payment at some future date. The main exception is the retail trade for a private individual.

Why is it necessary to record these transactions?

Even in the smallest business the proprietor or manager will want to have accurate and up-to-date information about how much has been bought and sold, how much money has been received for sales, how much has been paid away for purchases, etc. Private individuals often find it convenient to have the same information for their cash receipts and payments. You can imagine that with a very large business, chaos would quickly result without this information.

So bookkeeping really involves analysing in some way or another these various transactions?

You could say it involves recording these transactions so as to permit analysis in a systematic fashion, in a way that can be applied to all businesses of whatever kind, and that is intelligible not only now but at any future time.

Do you mean by this 'the double entry system of bookkeeping'?

Yes.

The term 'Books of Account' has a distinctly old-fashioned sound. It perhaps makes you think of a Charles Dickens novel set in early Victorian England, with rows of clerks perched on high stools writing in large books. Bookkeeping today is likely to be done with the aid of a computer rather than with handwritten books, and this is a virtual certainty in a business of any significance. Nevertheless, modern bookkeepers are doing exactly the same as the clerks in the Dickens novel, though they are doing it much more quickly and perhaps more accurately – though Victorian clerks achieved very high standards. (Whether or not they are any happier is a question for another book!)

The importance of bookkeeping

All businesses, without exception, need to keep accurate and readily accessible records of their financial transactions. Many organisations other than businesses also need to do it, and some individuals too. As a child I had a neighbour who died at the age of 75 leaving records that accounted for every penny of his income and expenditure since his 21st birthday. Surprisingly he was a charming, generous man and in no way a miser. Perhaps you too have a personal bookkeeping system to record your own financial affairs, though I would not recommend taking it to these extreme lengths.

The benefits to a business of dependable financial records are probably self-evident. They include:

- The law requires all companies and many other organisations to prepare accounts that conform with certain criteria. This can only be done if the basic, supporting financial records are in place.

- The tax authorities require it. If you do not believe me, try telling Her Majesty's Revenue and Customs that you cannot do a VAT return because you have not kept proper records.
- It is necessary to manage the bank account, cash and borrowing. Otherwise cheques might bounce or unproductive surpluses build up.
- Intelligently used, the records should warn of impending financial difficulties or even insolvency.
- Intelligently used, the records should provide the basis for efficiency savings and profitable business decisions.
- Without proper bookkeeping the owners would not know the worth of the business.
- It is, in many instances, essential in order to comply with money laundering regulations.

Single entry bookkeeping

As Julie Andrews memorably sang in *The Sound of Music*, the very beginning is a very good place to start, and single entry bookkeeping could be said to be the very beginning. In fact it is extremely basic, which is why it is not used by any business of significance. Some managers might think that they use it, but what actually happens is that the accountants take the books and documents away and convert them into double entry records.

Single entry bookkeeping is described here in order to show why double entry bookkeeping is almost universally used. However, a small body, such as perhaps a birdwatchers' club, just might use the single entry version. So might a sole trader or small partnership, provided that the accounts are not audited.

As the name suggests, single entry bookkeeping involves writing down each transaction just once. It is in fact the simple listing of money paid and received. Every time a cheque is written, the bookkeeper records in a book the date, the amount and the person or business being paid. Every time something is paid into the bank, the date, amount, and person or business from whom the money was received is recorded elsewhere in the book. Cash paid out and received is recorded in a similar way.

If the bookkeeper has been very careful, an accurate receipts and payments account can be prepared from the single entry records. It would, though, be wise to verify the figures as far as possible. After allowing for the starting balance, cash actually in the cash box should equal the cash received less the cash paid out. The balance on the bank statement should equal money banked less cheques written, after allowing for the opening balance and items that have not yet reached the statement.

Records kept in this way have severe limitations. Among them are:

- If a receipt or payment is entered in the book as an incorrect amount, the mistake may not be noticed.
- If the amount of a receipt or payment is entered correctly but the type of receipt or payment is wrongly classified, the mistake may not be noticed. It is only fair to say that this can also happen with double entry bookkeeping, though it is perhaps less likely.
- Money owing to or by the organisation is not shown. Just possibly nothing is owing to or by the organisation, but it is a severe limitation.
- Long-term assets are not shown. A car purchased two years ago for £20,000 does not appear at all in the records for the current year, even though it still has a significant value.
- Important things like depreciation and bad debts are not shown.

With considerable care it may be possible to prepare an accurate receipts and payments account, and this is certainly better than nothing, but double entry bookkeeping is much superior.

The concept of double entry bookkeeping

Double entry bookkeeping is much superior to single entry bookkeeping and all significant businesses keep their accounting records in this way. At the heart of double entry bookkeeping is the concept that every transaction involves both the giving of a benefit and the receiving of a benefit. Consequently, every transaction is written into the books twice, once as a debit and once as a credit. It follows that the bookkeeping system must always balance, which is a big advantage. Some types of mistake will cause the system to be out of balance, and as a result the bookkeeper will be alerted to a problem.

Double entry should not be taken to imply that two transactions are entered. It means that an inherent feature of a single transaction is that it is entered into two different accounts, in one as a debit and in one as a credit.

Consider as an example a cheque for £5,000 to insure the company cars. £5,000 is entered in the *Insurance Account* as a debit. This account will eventually be a charge in the profit and loss account. At the same time £5,000 will be credited to the *Bank Account*. This reduces the balance of money in the bank or increases the overdraft. The balance of the bank account will eventually appear in the balance sheet. Debits and credits are explained in the next section of this chapter.

Three basic rules of double entry bookkeeping

The founding father of double entry bookkeeping was a Franciscan monk called Luca Pacioli. He did not invent it, but in 1493 he wrote down the principles of the system being used by himself and others.

Given his calling he must have been a man of considerable education and wide-ranging interests. His work has stood the test of time because the fundamental principles are timeless. If he was able to visit a modern accounts office, once computers had been explained to him he would recognlse that his principles were still being applied.

The bookkeeping system (the ledger) will contain a number of accounts, perhaps just a few or perhaps many thousands. The previous section of this chapter gave an example of a cheque for £5,000 paying an insurance premium. This resulted in postings to the Insurance Account and the Bank Account. Each account has a separate page in the ledger, though in practice the records are likely to be computerised. In a manual system the layout of each account will be the same. The following show the two entries resulting from the payment of the insurance premium.

Insurance Account

Debit					Credit
Date	Details	Amount	Date	Details	Amount
		£			£
4 April	Bank	5,000			

Bank Account

Debit					Credit
Date	Details	Amount	Date	Details	Amount
		£			£
			4 April	Bank	5,000

As you look at these accounts please keep in mind:

- They might seem rather cramped, but in reality the paper would almost certainly be considerably wider than this book.
- Debit is often abbreviated to 'Dr' and Credit is often abbreviated to 'Cr'.

- The entry may incorporate a folio reference. This is not shown but it enables each entry to be cross-referenced to the correct input document.

It is time now to list and explain three fundamental rules that apply today and which Luca Pacioli would undoubtedly recognise.

1. Debit on the left, credit on the right

Why this way round? It does not matter so long as everyone does it the same way. It is rather like driving – it does not matter which side of the road we drive so long as everyone follows the same law or convention. A long time ago most people did it this way, so that's the way we all do it.

On my first morning as a trainee accountant I was told that debit was nearest the window and that it was best not to talk to the boss until he had had a cup of tea. I found both pieces of advice invaluable, but I always sat with my left shoulder next to the glass.

2. Debit receives the benefit, credit gives the benefit

Again, why this way round? Again, because it was decided a long time ago and that's the way it is. The rule may be hard to grasp and it is probably the opposite of what you would instinctively expect. After all your bank statement is credited when money is paid into your bank account. But look at it from the bank's point of view, and it is the bank that issues the statement. The bank's records are a mirror image of your records, so a credit for the bank is a debit for you, and vice versa.

It may help you to remember the rule if you keep in mind that assets in the balance sheet and costs in the profit and loss account are both debits. So if you buy a new factory or if you buy some postage stamps, the appropriate accounts will be debited. Liabilities in the balance sheet and income in the profit and loss account are both credits. So if you buy something on credit, the amount is credited to the supplier's account. This is because it is a liability. Similarly, if you make a sale, the amount is credited to sales account and it will eventually contribute to revenue in the profit and loss account. It is all explained further in the next chapter.

3. For every debit there must be a credit

This is a fundamental and implicit consequence of double entry bookkeeping, and there are no exceptions. One account gives the benefit and one account receives the benefit. Scientists sometimes help themselves remember the rule by thinking of the law of physics: *'for every action there is an equal and opposite reaction'*.

We have already seen how this works in relation to the insurance premium payment of £5,000, but it is not always so straightforward. In fact it may be exceedingly complicated. A batch of postings may include a large number of debits and credits, but the total of the debits must always equal the total of the credits. If they do not, a mistake has been made. As an example consider the entries resulting from an approved expense claim. The amounts are large, so perhaps the expenses were incurred by a senior manager or just possibly a journalist.

	£
Travel	806
Hotel costs	1,294
Meals	317
Entertaining	3,994
Telephone	88
	6,499

Five individual accounts would be debited with a total of £6,499. One account would be credited with £6,499.

So please remember the first fundamental rule of double entry bookkeeping: *'for every debit there must be a credit'.* There are no exceptions and it ranks alongside 'The sun always rises in the east', 'Water does not flow uphill' and 'A Government initiative to cut bureaucracy always creates extra work'.

Two examples of double entry bookkeeping postings

This section of the chapter illustrates with two practical examples the principles already explained. The first is extremely straightforward. In the section about single entry bookkeeping the point was made that a birdwatchers' club might not see the need for double entry records, but let us suppose that a new treasurer has instituted a double entry system and that the following four events occur on the first day:

- A member pays her annual subscription of £50.
- The club buys a new telescope for £400.
- The treasurer is reimbursed £100 for stamps that he has bought.
- The annual subscription of £75 is paid to The Federation of British Birdwatchers.

Bank Account

Debit		£	Credit	£
Subscriptions Received		50	Equipment	400
			Postage	100
			Subscriptions Paid	75

Subscriptions Received Account

Debit		£	Credit	£
			Bank	50

Equipment Account

Debit		£	Credit	£
Bank		400		

Postage Account

Debit		£	Credit	£
Bank		100		

Subscriptions Paid Account

Debit		£	Credit	£
Bank		75		

You will no doubt have noticed that the debits have received the benefits and that the credits have given the benefits, and also that the total of the debits equals the total of the credits. You may also have noticed that more has gone out of the bank than has been received. Let us hope that the birdwatchers have an agreed overdraft facility or started the period with money in the bank.

The second example relates to a business and involves purchases and sales made on credit. The accounts reflect the posting for the following transactions.

- A sale of £110 is made for cash which is banked.
- A sale of £4,000 is made on credit to J. K. Patel Ltd.
- A sale of £60 is made on credit to Cohen and Levin Ltd.
- Payment of £3,200 (relating to a previous sale) is received from J. K. Patel Ltd.
- Widgets for resale costing £2,700 are purchased on credit from Widget Supplies Ltd.
- Wages of £6,000 are paid.
- An invoice for £2,000 relating to advertising is received from King Brothers.

Bank Account

Debit	£	Credit	£
Sales	110	Wages	6,000
J. K. Patel Ltd.	3,200		

Sales Account

Debit	£	Credit	£
		Bank Account	110
		J. K. Patel Ltd	4,000
		Cohen and Levin Ltd	60

J. K. Patel Ltd

Debit	£	Credit	£
Sales	4,000	Bank Account	3,200

Cohen and Levin Ltd

Debit	£	Credit	£
Sales	60		

Stock Account

Debit	£	Credit	£
Widget Supplies Ltd.	2,700		

Widget Supplies Ltd

Debit	£	Credit	£
		Stock	2,700

Wages Account

Debit	£	Credit	£
Bank Account	6,000		

Advertising

Debit	£	Credit	£
King Brothers	2,000		

King Brothers

Debit	£	Credit	£
		Advertising	2,000

Questions to test your understanding

1. Does credit give the benefit or receive the benefit?
2. The treasurer of Kidwilton Village Football Club keeps the books using a double entry system. Write up the accounts to reflect the following transactions:

- Annual subscriptions of £50 are received in cash from each of four members and the money is banked.
- Rent of £500 is paid to the farmer who owns the football field.
- An invoice from a firm of solicitors (Lafferty and Reed) is received. The amount is £300.
- An invoice from a printer (K. Klaus Ltd) is received. The amount is £170.
- A donation of £5,000 is received from the club's president. The cheque is banked.

INSTANT TIP

For every debit there must be a credit. If there is not, a mistake has been made.

02

What are the different types of account and different ledgers?

This chapter extends your knowledge of bookkeeping principles by explaining the sales and purchase ledgers that are kept outside the main ledger. This main ledger, which is often known as the nominal ledger, is explained in more detail, and the various posting mediums are explained. Most importantly we recognise that there are five different types of account within the nominal ledger, although entries may freely be posted between them. The topics covered are:

- The five different types of account.
- The nominal ledger.
- The books of prime entry.
- The nominal journal (or just journal).
- The sales ledger.
- The sales day book.
- The purchase ledger.
- The purchase day book.

The five different types of account

The five different types of account are explained in this section. They are all in the main nominal ledger and, despite their different features, entries may be posted freely between them. To repeat key points made in the last chapter, this must be done with debit receiving the benefit and credit giving the benefit, and with the total of the debits equalling the total of the credits. The five different accounts are treated differently when the accounts are prepared. They are:

Income accounts

These relate to sales or other income and they increase the profit. They almost always have a credit balance and are eventually credited to the profit and loss account. Of course, if goods are returned for a refund, there will be a debit to an income account.

In the last chapter the sale of £4,000 to J. K. Patel Ltd was credited to an income account. The other side of the posting went to an asset account.

Expenditure accounts

These accounts are made up of expenditure that reduces the profit. They almost always have a debit balance and are eventually debited to the profit and loss account.

In the last chapter the £2,000 invoice from King Brothers went into an expenditure account. The other side of the posting went to a liability account.

Asset accounts

These accounts normally have a debit balance and are made up of assets that retain their value. This is distinct from say the electricity account which is an expenditure account. Examples of asset accounts are stock, motor vehicles and bank accounts (if there is not an overdraft). Money owing to the business is in debtor accounts and these are asset accounts. Asset accounts eventually go into the balance sheet, not the profit and loss account.

In the last chapter the £2,700 for widgets went into stock, which is an asset account. The other side of the posting went to a liability account.

Liability accounts

These accounts are the debts of the business and they normally have a credit balance. Examples are the accounts for money owing to suppliers and these accounts are called creditors. A further example is the bank account (if there is an overdraft). Liability accounts eventually go into the balance sheet, not the profit and loss account.

In the last chapter the £2,000 invoice from King Brothers was credited to a liability account. The other side of the posting went to an expenditure account.

Capital accounts

These accounts represent the investment in the business by the owners. If the business is a company, it is the net worth owned by the shareholders. It might be hard to grasp but it is true for all businesses, even a sole trader. If the capital accounts in Deborah

Fountain's hat making business total £7,000, then this is her investment in the business. She could take the £7,000 out, close the business down and go on holiday. The business is separate from the person who owns it. An example of a capital account is Revenue Reserves.

If the business makes profits after tax, and disregarding dividends and other distributions, the value of the capital accounts will increase over time. So long as a business is solvent the capital accounts will have credit balances. A net debit balance is a desperate sign of trouble and often means that the closing of the business is imminent.

All this is illustrated by the following ten commonly used accounts. Marked by the side of each is whether they usually have a debit or credit balance and the type of account that they are.

Account name	Debit/credit balance	Type of account
Fixtures and fittings	normally debit balance	asset account
Salaries	normally debit balance	expenditure account
Legal and professional expenses	normally debit balance	expenditure account
Revenue reserves	normally credit balance	capital account
Share capital	normally credit balance	capital account
Trade debtors	normally debit balance	asset account
Trade creditors	normally credit balance	liability account
Hire purchase creditors	normally credit balance	liability account
Shop takings	normally credit balance	income account
Goods sold	normally credit balance	income account

The nominal ledger

The nominal ledger is the principal ledger. Other ledgers may be kept, particularly a sales ledger and a purchase ledger, and in a sizeable business this is very likely, but each one will be a subsidiary ledger and reconcile to a control account in the nominal ledger. This means that, for example, the net total of thousands of accounts in the sales ledger add to just one figure which is a single account in the nominal ledger. According to circumstances other subsidiary ledgers may be kept. An example is a listing of the various fixed asset accounts.

The nominal ledger may be very big, perhaps containing thousands of individual accounts. This will certainly be the case for a major company and it is therefore necessary to have a system for coding and grouping the accounts.

In a simple system the accounts will just be listed, probably in alphabetical order. In a more complex system they will be grouped in a logical manner. For example, if there are several different bank accounts they may be listed next to each other. This is convenient and when the balance sheet is prepared all the bank accounts will be added to the one total that will appear in it. Similarly, it is usual to group all the overhead expenditure accounts by department.

In all but the very smallest systems, it is normal to give each account an identifying number. This is quicker to write out and if the system is mechanised or computerised, the person posting the entries will post according to the numbers only.

There are thousands of different accounting numbering systems and you may want to design your own to fit your business and individual circumstances. It is worth looking at the numbering system of your employer or some other organisation. Whether or not it is a good system, make sure that you understand the principles of the numbering.

The books of prime entry

It is possible to write all entries directly into the nominal ledger without using subsidiary books at all. This is sometimes done, especially in very small businesses, but there are two major drawbacks:

- Unless the business is exceedingly small the main nominal ledger will become clogged up with a very large number of entries.
- It is a good idea to record a certain amount of detail about each entry, and not just the amount and the name of the account that completes the double entry. There just is not room in the nominal ledger for the necessary details.

It is good practice to post to the nominal ledger only from the books of prime entry. The necessary details should be recorded in these books and it is usually just totals that are posted to the nominal ledger. There are a number of books that may be encountered but the following three are used in most businesses and are examined in this chapter:

- The nominal journal (or just journal).
- The sales day book.
- The purchase day book.

The term 'day book' is used because it may, in theory at least, be totalled and posted daily. The cash book is another book of prime entry and this is examined in the next chapter.

The nominal journal (or just journal)

Although there may be other books of prime entry, it is likely that the great majority of postings to the nominal ledger will be made by means of three of them, namely the sales day book, the purchase day book and the cash book. This will inevitably leave a number of necessary postings, probably important but relatively small in number, that do not fit into any of these posting mediums. As already explained, it is not a good idea to post directly into the nominal ledger without a posting medium. Apart from anything else some narrative details are highly desirable, to reduce the risk of fraud, to assist auditors and to provide a trail of information for the bookkeeper and the managers. This leaves the nominal journal.

The journal is ruled to show the date, a reference number for the entry, the identity of the accounts to be debited and credited, the amounts to be debited and credited and a narrative explanation. An example of a journal entry is as follows:

		Debit	Credit
1 March	Bad debts written off	£1,000.00	
JV99	Curzon & Co.		£1,000.00

To write off bad debt following bankruptcy of customer.

This implies that the customer's account (Curzon & Co) is actually in the nominal ledger but, of course, it is much more likely to be in a separate sales ledger. If this is the case, the journal entry would be to credit the sales ledger control account and a separate posting must be made in the sales ledger. A computerised system will make the second posting automatically.

You will no doubt have noticed that the journal is not laid out like a ledger sheet. This is because it is not a ledger sheet. It is a book of prime entry. It is possible that you may encounter a journal with a slightly different layout. There is more than one view about what is exactly best.

This section of the chapter is completed by showing how three events are written in the journal. The three events are:

1. It is noticed that an invoice for £76 from J. L. Lafferty Ltd has wrongly been debited to Printing and Stationery Account instead of Motor Expenses Account. The invoice was entered on 4 January as part of Purchase Day Book Batch 66.
2. Interest of £9 (at an annual rate of 5%) for the year to 28 February is charged to the Director's Loan Account.

3. Annual depreciation of 25% is posted relating to Ford Mondeo XRJ 617. This relates to the year to 28 February and the car was purchased two years ago for £16,000.

		Debit £	Credit £
28 Feb.	Printing and Stationery		76
JV179	Motor Expenses	76	
	To correct misposting of invoice from J. L. Lafferty Ltd entered on 4 January in Purchase Day Book Batch 66.		
28 Feb	Interest received		9
JV180	Director's Loan Account	9	
	Interest on Director's Loan Account at 5% for the year to 28 February.		
28 Feb JV181	Depreciation on motor vehicles		4,000
	Depreciation	4,000	
	Depreciation charge at 25% pa on Ford Mondeo XRJ 617 for year to 28 February.		

It is important that each journal entry has a reference number so that it can be readily identified. There are numerous reference number possibilities but JV (standing for Journal Voucher) or just J is often used. It is very likely that each nominal account mentioned will have an identifying reference number. This was explained earlier in this chapter in the section on the nominal ledger. In real life the narrative would mention the year as well as the day and month.

The entry relating to depreciation may need a little explanation, though the subject is covered in detail in Chapter 6. The debit to Depreciation Account will increase the amount debited to the profit and loss account. The credit to Depreciation on Motor Vehicles Account builds up a credit balance to offset the £16,000 debit balance in the balance sheet. After four years the motor vehicle will have a nil value in the balance sheet, represented by £16,000 debit and £16,000 credit.

The sales ledger

If you only have one customer, you will not need a detailed sales ledger, just one account in the nominal ledger. Nor will you need a sales ledger if your sales are entirely for cash. On the other hand, businesses that sell on credit may have many customers. For them, an efficient sales ledger outside the nominal ledger is essential.

A sales ledger account looks very like a nominal ledger account. It is divided in the middle with debit on the left and credit on the right. There will be one account for each customer and the postings to it are:

Debit	invoices issued
Credit	credit notes issued
Credit	cash received
Credit	invoices written off as bad debts

Normally the debits on each account will exceed the credits. This means that the account has a debit balance which is the amount owed to the business by the customers. This sum is represented by just one account (usually called the sales ledger control account) in the nominal system.

The bookkeeping system will be designed to ensure that the accounts in the sales ledger do actually add up to the balance of the control account. Sales ledger accounts ruled in the traditional way described may not be encountered too often, though they are still used. Many readers will only be familiar with computer printouts that do not look anything like the ledgers described. It is important to remember that a computer is just an efficient way of doing what could be done manually.

Some of the figures on the computer printout represent credits and some represent debits. They are just presented differently. It is worth proving this to yourself by marking the debits and credits on a computerised sales ledger.

A business needs to send out statements and operate credit control procedures. These are a by-product of the sales ledgers and a computerised system speeds up the process. A computerised system may operate on the open item principle. This means that cash payments are allocated to specific invoices, and customer statements only show unpaid invoices. A computerised system may readily give useful management information such as an ageing of the debts.

The sales day book

It is necessary to have a mechanism for posting sales invoices into the sales ledger and the nominal ledger. This could be done laboriously one by one, but it is better to group them together and cut down the work.

This posting medium is usually called the sales day book, though you might find it called the sales journal or some other name. The following is a typical example of a sales day book. However, the design can vary according to individual preference and business circumstances.

Date	Customer	Invoice no.	Folio no.	Goods total £	VAT £	Invoice total £
1 June	Bigg and Son	1001	B4	100.00	17.50	117.50
4 June	Carter Ltd	1002	C1	200.00	35.00	235.00
12 June	XYZ Ltd	1003	X1	50.00	8.75	58.75
17 June	Martin Bros.	1004	M2	100.00	17.50	117.50
26 June	Fishers Ltd	1005	F5	10.00	1.75	11.75
30 June	Dawson Ltd	1006	D2	20.00	3.50	23.50
				480.00	84.00	564.00

Please note the following about each column:

- *Date* This is the date of each individual invoice.
- *Customer* This is the customer to which each individual invoice is addressed.
- *Invoice no.* Each invoice must be individually numbered
- *Folio no.* This is the identifying code to each individual sales ledger account.
- *Goods total* This is the total value of each invoice excluding VAT. Sometimes this is further divided to include different totals for different product groups. The example given only shows total sales.
- *VAT* This is the VAT charged on each individual invoice.
- *Invoice total* This is the total amount of each individual invoice and the amount that the customer has to pay.

The columns may be added and the posting done whenever it is convenient to do so. Monthly posting is frequently encountered and in practice there would probably be more than six invoices. The posting to the nominal ledger would be:

Sales account   £480.00 credit   The sales account will eventually contribute to profit in the profit and loss account.

VAT account	£84.00 credit	This is a liability account. It is money owed by the business to the government.
Sales ledger control account	£564.00 debit	This is an asset account. It is money owing to the business by customers.

Six individual sales ledger accounts are debited with the total amount of the six individual invoices. You will notice that the balances of the sales ledger accounts will add up to the value of the sales ledger control account in the nominal ledger.

If you have a computerised system, your records will probably not look like this example. The computer will follow exactly these principles and do the same job, but it will do it more quickly.

The purchase ledger

If you have thoroughly understood the section on the sales ledger you will have no trouble at all understanding this section on the purchase ledger. This is because the purchase ledger is a mirror image of the sales ledger. It is used for invoices submitted to the business by suppliers.

The layout is similar to the accounts in the nominal ledger and the sales ledger. Postings to it are:

Credit	suppliers' invoices received
Debit	suppliers' credit notes received
Debit	cash payments made

Each account will normally have a credit balance and this represents the amount owing to the supplier by the business. The total of all the individual purchase ledger accounts is the same as the amount of the purchase ledger control account in the nominal ledger. Customers will submit statements to you and press you to make regular prompt payments to them.

The purchase day book

We have already seen that the purchase ledger is a mirror image of the sales ledger. You will therefore not be surprised to learn that the purchases day book is a mirror image of the sales day book. Do not be confused if you find it called the purchases journal or some other name, and do not be confused if it is a computerised system with a layout that makes sense to computer experts.

A typical purchase day book looks like the following:

Date	Customer	Invoice no.	Folio no.	Goods total £	VAT £	Invoice total £
1 July	Jones Ltd	3001	J8	100.00	17.50	117.50
9 July	King and Co.	3002	K3	300.00	52.50	352.50
13 July	ABC Ltd	3003	A1	50.00	8.75	58.75
20 July	Dodd & Carr	3004	D2	200.00	35.00	235.00
28 July	Sugar Co. Ltd	3005	S8	30.00	5.25	35.25
				680.00	119.00	799.00

The purchase day book is the medium through which a batch of suppliers' invoices is posted into the nominal system and into the purchase ledger. It avoids the need to enter them individually into the nominal system. It is usually ruled off and entered monthly but this can be done at any suitable interval.

Questions to test your understanding

1. In which of the five categories should each of the following ten accounts be listed? For each one show whether it normally has a debit balance or a credit balance, and whether it will go to the profit and loss account or the balance sheet.

   - Plant and machinery
   - Sales
   - Wages
   - Capital reserves
   - Cash
   - Telephone
   - Computer equipment
   - Bank account (with an overdraft)
   - Six Per Cent Preference Shares
   - Rent

2. What is the function of the sales ledger control account?

3. Do you need a sales ledger if your sales are entirely for cash?

4. Write up the nominal journal entries made necessary by the following events:

   - A decision is made on 4 June that a balance of £777 owing by F. Smith Ltd is wholly irrecoverable and should be treated as a bad debt. The company operates a sales ledger separate from the nominal ledger.
   - A decision is taken on 4 June that a general bad debt reserve of £6,000 should be created.

INSTANT TIP

The narrative description in the journal should not be neglected. To do so may well cause difficulties later.

03

What should I know about cash and reconciliations?

Accountants frequently use the term 'cash' to cover both bank accounts and physical cash, namely notes and coins, and, as you will probably know, in most businesses the bank accounts have much the greater significance. The first part of this chapter deals with the bookkeeping implications of cash, and, of course, the cash book is one of the books of prime entry. It is important and the great significance of cash is made clear in later chapters. For the same reason the bank reconciliation, which is also covered in this chapter, should on no account be neglected.

Running short of working capital and cash can be very damaging to a business, or even fatal. Perhaps surprisingly, it is not uncommon for a failed business to be making profits at the time of the failure. The proper and timely maintenance of the bookkeeping records can be of great assistance in preventing this, and it is of course sound practice for other reasons too. The topics covered in this chapter are:

- The cash book.
- Petty cash.
- The bank reconciliation.
- Other reconciliations.

The cash book

Almost any set of accounting records involves the receiving and paying out of money, sometimes cheques, sometimes cash and sometimes both. If there are only a very few entries, it may all be recorded in the bank account and cash account in the nominal ledger, but due to the number of entries it is usual to maintain a separate cash book. Sometimes bank and cash are combined in one book and sometimes two books are kept.

As the cash books are a medium of posting to the nominal ledger they are books of prime entry. Sometimes the cash book is just a posting medium and sometimes a running balance is maintained as an integral part of the system.

The cash book will have two sides, one for payments and one for receipts. The following is an example of the payments side of a cash book maintained for bank entries.

Date	Cheque no.	Payee	Folio	Amount £
4 May	1234	Simpson and Co.	S3	200.68
9 May	1235	Jones Ltd	J8	33.11
14 May	–	Bank charges	39	10.00
17 May	1236	Wainrights	W1	111.00
19 May	1237	Cubitt Ltd	C9	44.00
				398.79

The total of £398.79 would be credited to the bank account in the nominal ledger (remember payments out of a bank account are credits). Various accounts are debited and these are identified by the folio numbers.

In reality there may be hundreds of entries or perhaps many more. The posting may be made easier by analysing the payment amounts over extra columns. If there are three entries for bank charges, only the total of the bank charges need be posted, rather than three individual items. The following exceptionally simple illustration shows how three extra columns could be added in support of the above five payments.

Amount £	Stationery £	Legal and professional £	Bank charges £
200.68		200.68	
33.11	33.11		
10.00			10.00
111.00		111.00	
44.00	44.00		
398.79	77.11	311.68	10.00

This means that only three debits need be posted instead of five. In a significant business the reduction in the number of postings might be very large.

There will be a corresponding side for the receipts, but as the principles are the same it is not necessary to show an illustration. The next example (see page 32) shows a full cash book balanced at the month end.

The folios identify the accounts to be posted as the opposite side of the double entry. Various identification systems may be encountered but you will probably have no difficulty realising that SL means sales ledger and that PL means purchase ledger.

This is a completed cash book for the month of September and the book has been ruled off and balanced. The balancing may be done at any time but once a month is typical. It is done by adding the columns and writing in the difference on the side that has the smaller of the two figures. This is expressed as the balance carried down. The two columns then add to the same amount. The balancing figure is then transferred to the other column and becomes the opening balance in the next period.

RECEIPTS

Date		Folio	Amount £
1 Sept	Balance	b/d	800.00
4 Sept	Cross and Co.	SL6	101.10
9 Sept	Figg Ltd	SL12	17.11
13 Sept	Morgan Ltd	SL17	34.19
18 Sept	Peters and Brown	SL3	700.00
30 Sept	Trapp Ltd	SL22	1,091.00
			2,743.40
1 Oct	Balance	b/d	1,006.90

PAYMENTS

Date			Folio	Amount £
1 Sept	4001	Arkwright	PL3	29.16
2 Sept	4002	Rates	NL4	290.00
6 Sept	4003	Stevens Ltd	PL7	34.12
9 Sept	4004	Wilson Bros	PL19	47.11
12 Sept	4005	Crabbe and Co.	PL8	39.12
17 Sept	4006	Carter	PL2	200.00
19 Sept	4007	Jenkins	PL12	56.99
23 Sept	4008	Champion and Co.	PL17	450.00
24 Sept	4009	Wages	NL4	290.00
29 Sept	4010	Barton and Hicks	PL1	300.00
30 Sept	Balance		c/d	1,006.90
				2,743.40

In the example the balance brought down (b/d) on 1 September is on the receipts side which means that there is money in the bank and no overdraft. This is still the position when the account is balanced on 30 September.

The four figure numbers before the names on the payments side are cheque numbers. This is optional and will assist when the bank reconciliation is done.

Following (see page 34) is an extremely simple example of a cash book that combines both cash entries and bank entries. It shows receipts and payments for both and it is balanced for both. For the sake of simplicity the pence have been omitted and only the pounds are shown.

Finally it should be mentioned that cash books sometimes incorporate discount columns. This is for discounts deducted by customers because they have paid within the permitted period, and for discounts deducted from payments by the business for the same reason. In practice, as you may know, settlement discount is often deducted although the settlement terms have not been properly observed. Policing the system causes many practical problems and dilemmas. Sales managers are often reluctant to have their customers annoyed by requests for additional payments.

Cash Book

RECEIPTS

Date		Folio	Cash £	Bank £
6 Aug	M Jones Ltd	J6		329
10 Aug	P Lydd Ltd	L9		472
14 Aug	K and T Smith	S42	300	
18 Aug	Broadway Supplies Ltd	B18		219
27 Aug	John Crabbe	C11	406	
29 Aug	Turville Products	T7	201	
30 Aug	Tring Parker Ltd	T6		661
			907	1,681
1 Sept	Balances b/d		224	302

PAYMENTS

Date		Folio	Cash £	Bank £
1 Aug	Balances b/d		42	806
8 Aug	J. White Ltd	W4		101
15 Aug	F. Carr Ltd	C5	222	
19 Aug	Brown Brothers	B12		116
30 Aug	L. Peters Ltd	P4		356
31 Aug	Adams and Dennis	A1	419	
31 Aug	Balance c/d		224	302
			907	1,681

Petty cash

Cash payments may be recorded as part of the main cash book which was described in the last section of this chapter. However, there may be a petty cash book as well. Petty cash is used for cash payments and among other things it groups entries for input into the nominal ledger. It may just record the petty cash payments but the imprest system is generally used. The word 'petty' means small or trivial, and the purpose of the petty cash system is to allow small and trivial disbursements to be made. This limitation may not always be apparent to colleagues who may try to obtain large sums of money from it. Nevertheless, the purpose is to handle small sums of money.

A typical petty cash book is very wide, has two sides, and has a considerable number of columns for analysis. This makes it difficult to reproduce here but the following is a simplified example of how the payments side typically looks:

Date	Details of expense	Voucher no.	Total £	Stamps £	Petrol £
2 May	Stamps	1	10.00	10.00	
16 May	Petrol	2	18.48		18.48
29 May	Stamps	3	10.00	10.00	
			38.48	20.00	18.48
May	Balance c/d		11.52		
			50.00		

In practice there would of course be many more entries and a further dozen or so analysis columns to record the different categories of expense (milk, stationery, etc). The total column is always used and this is the total amount paid out on each voucher. If someone is claiming £10 for stamps and £10 for petrol, then £20 would be entered in the total column.

The example assumes that the imprest system is in use and that the float is £50.00. This operates by a specified sum of money, £50.00 or some such figure, being given to the petty cashier when the petty cash system is established. At the end of the week or month the total amount expended is reimbursed, so that the float is restored to the original sum. The imprest system is preferred by auditors and is much superior to other systems.

Under the imprest system the amount of money in the petty cash box, plus the payments made and recorded in the book, should add up to the amount of the float. If they do not, a mistake has been made. In the example a cheque for £38.48 would be written and cashed. This would restore the float to £50 and this would be the opening balance for June. The accounting entries to record the May transactions would be:

Postage account	£20.00 debit
Petrol account	£18.48 debit
Petty cash account	£38.48 credit

The entry for the reimbursement cheque would be:

Petty cash account	£38.48 debit
Bank account	£38.48 credit

After all the entries have been posted, the petty cash account should have a balance of £50 in debit in the nominal ledger. It is an asset account and there is £50 cash to support it. A £50 cheque would have been written on Day 1.

The bank reconciliation

It is important that the cash book (or bank account in the nominal ledger) is regularly reconciled to the bank statement. It is suggested that this be done at least monthly and perhaps more frequently. It should certainly be done at the balance sheet date.

The writer Ernest Hemingway often did not bother to bank cheques that he received, preferring instead to use them as bookmarks. After his death his house was found to contain many unbanked cheques, some as much as 20 years old. Although the cheques were very seriously out of date many of them were subsequently honoured. This is an extreme example of why the bank statement balance might not be the same as the cash book balance and why it is necessary to reconcile the two figures. Such bizarre behaviour is unlikely in businesses, but bank reconciliations are necessary to show that mistakes have not been made (if this is the case), to identify any errors so that they can be corrected, and to properly control the cash resources and borrowing.

Possible reasons for differences in the two figures to be reconciled are:

- Cheques written in the cash book have not yet been debited to the bank statement.
- Receipts written in the cash book have not yet been credited to the bank statement.
- Items have been debited to the bank statement that have not yet been written in the cash book. Common examples are direct debits, standing orders and bank charges.
- Receipts have been credited to the bank statement that have not yet been written in the cash book. This could for example include a receipt from a customer paid directly to the bank account by the BACS system.
- You have made a mistake. Perhaps the wrong amount has been written into the cash book or a paying-in slip has been added incorrectly.
- The bank has made a mistake. This is unlikely, but it can happen. Cynics might think that it is more likely now than in past years.

The task of preparing the bank reconciliation should be approached in a methodical manner. The bank statement should be ticked to the cash book, then any differences should be noted, investigated and written down logically. If it is done correctly, the two figures will reconcile. This is, of course, provided that the opening balances reconciled. This is another way of saying that the bank reconciliation at the end of the previous period was correct.

This is best illustrated with an example. The following is a simplified bank statement for the company whose cash book was reproduced earlier in this chapter. It is for September, corresponding with the period covered by the cash book. As it is a bank statement, receipts are printed on the right, the opposite side to the normal cash book layout.

Date	Detail	Payments £	Receipts £	Balance £
1 Sept	Opening balance			800.00 cr
6 Sept	Counter credit		101.10	
6 Sept	4001	29.16		
6 Sept	4002	290.00		581.94 cr
11 Sept	Counter credit		17.11	599.05 cr
12 Sept	Direct debit – gas	105.16		493.89 cr
15 Sept	Counter credit		34.19	
15 Sept	4003	34.12		
15 Sept	4004	47.11		
15 Sept	Direct debit – electricity	61.82		385.03 cr
20 Sept	Counter credit		700.00	
20 Sept	Credit transfer received		349.21	1,434.24 cr
21 Sept	4005	38.12		1,396.12 cr
30 Sept	4008	450.00		946.12 cr

The bank reconciliation is as follows:

Cash book balance at 30 September		1,006.90 dr
Add cheques not yet presented		
4006	200.00	
4007	56.99	
4009	290.00	
4010	300.00	
	846.99	
		1,853.89
Add credit on statement not in cash book		349.21
		2,203.10
Less receipt in cash book not on statement		1,091.00
		1,112.10
Less payments on statement not in cash book		
Direct debit – gas	105.16	
Direct debit – electricity	61.82	
		166.98
		945.12
Add difference to be investigated (cheque 4005 for £39.12 entered by bank as £38.12)		1.00
As per bank statement balance at 30 September		946.12 dr

Other reconciliations

A good bookkeeper will at least periodically, and perhaps frequently, reconcile various accounts in the bookkeeping system. A primary purpose is to prove (as far as possible) that everything is in order or, if mistakes have been made, to identify them and correct them. Reconciliations may help deter or reduce the consequences of fraud, and will please the auditors. Reconciliations are particularly important at the balance sheet date as a step in preparing the accounts.

The following are among the reconciliations that should be considered:

- The total of the sales ledger accounts should be reconciled with the sales ledger control account.
- The total of the purchase ledger accounts should be reconciled with the purchase ledger control account.
- The existence of the fixed assets should be verified and checked against the fixed asset accounts in the nominal ledger.
- Stock should be checked and agreed with the stock accounts in the nominal ledger.
- The corporation tax account should be reconciled. The corporation tax entries are normally made before the tax payable has been agreed with HMRC and sometimes more than one year may be 'open'. In any case, payments will be made at various dates. The agreed amounts owing (or the latest best estimates) should be reconciled with the corporation tax account in the nominal ledger.

Other possibilities include reconciliations relating to PAYE and national insurance, and also to VAT.

Important as the reconciliations are, it should not be forgotten that they will not necessarily reveal all types of mistakes. Compensating errors and a figure debited or credited to a wrong account (such as A. Smith Ltd instead of E. Smith Ltd, both in the sales ledger) are particularly hard to find.

Finally mention should be made of our old friend the suspense account. Nearly all bookkeeping systems have one of these and various things are debited or credited to it for a variety of reasons. Just one of numerous possibilities is a lack of information about a cheque that has been banked. In order to complete the double entry the suspense account would be credited pending an investigation.

It is sometimes claimed that computerised systems cut down the number of entries in the suspense account and make it impossible for the total of the debits not to equal the total of the credits. This last claim is certainly true, but you are still advised to be cautious and reconcile thoroughly. Some computerised systems will accept entries that do not balance, and achieve balance by putting the difference into a suspense account. Remember the adage GIGO, which stands for 'Garbage In Garbage Out'. Suspense accounts should be regularly reconciled, and the component entries identified and investigated. By definition a suspense account is only a temporary home, so the constituent parts must be journalled out to their final and rightful home.

Questions to test your understanding

1. Would you expect a bank reconciliation to disclose a compensating error?
2. Prepare a bank reconciliation as at 30 June. The bank statement for the month is as follows:

Date	Detail	Payments £	Receipts £	Balance £
1 June	Opening balance			62.61 cr
2 June	Counter credit		134.99	197.60 cr
9 June	Counter credit		801.11	998.71 cr
9 June	Direct debit	127.41		871.30 cr
12 June	Charges	117.48		753.82 cr
18 June	317	364.27		389.55 cr
23 June	318	616.24		226.69 dr
30 June	Counter credit		1,400.22	1,173.53 cr

The bank reconciliation at 30 May was as follows:

Cash book balance at 31 May	112.61 dr
Less charges on statement not in cash book	50.00
As per bank statement balance at 31 May	62.61 dr

The cash book for the month of June is as follows on page 42:

CASH BOOK

RECEIPTS Date		Folio	Amount £	PAYMENTS Date		Folio		Amount £
1 June	Balance	b/d	112.61	4 June	D.D.	L. Peters	P3	127.41
2 June	Morgan and Co.	M6	134.99	4 June	316	K. Brown Ltd	B5	77.22
9 June	J. Redding Ltd	R7	801.11	12 June	CHS	Bank charges	NL	50.00
30 June	Church and Partners	C3	1,400.22	12 June	317	Pound Ltd	P11	364.27
30 June	Figgin Products Ltd	F4	720.66	19 June	318	Jeffreys Ltd	J8	616.24
				21 June	319	F Green Ltd	G6	16.12
				29 June	320	Stone and Co.	S9	17.81
				30 June	321	XYZ Ltd.	X1	44.44
			3,169.59	30 June		Balance	c/d	1,856.08
								3,169.59
1 July	Balance	b/d	1,856.08					

INSTANT TIP

Approach reconciliations in a methodical manner. Remember what you were probably told as a child, 'Cool, calm deliberation untangles every knot'.

04

What other matters affect the bookkeeping records?

We will soon be ready to move on to the preparation of the accounts but first it is necessary to look at three major features of many bookkeeping systems. They should be understood because they are important and also because they generate some rather special entries. The chapter also deals with the important topic of the trial balance and the list of subjects is:

- Stock.
- Value added tax.
- Payroll and associated matters.
- The trial balance.

There is inevitably some law involved in the subjects of value added tax and payroll. For the purposes of these sections, UK law is exclusively used. This should be kept in mind if you operate in a territory other than the UK. Value added tax is administered and collected by Customs and Excise, which is part of Her Majesty's Revenue and Customs. The name of this august and revered institution is often shortened to HMRC and I have used this term extensively in the chapter.

Stock

Businesses operate by selling goods, services or both. A business that only sells services does not account for stock, but businesses that sell goods (either bought in or manufactured by itself) must keep stock accounts and should carry out periodic stocktakes.

The following is a simplified summary of the accounts associated with stock:

Stock account

The cost of goods purchased or manufactured is debited to this account, which is of course an asset account. This cost is transferred out when the goods are sold, scrapped or otherwise disposed of.

Returns inwards account

This is for the cost of goods returned to the business by its customers. The appropriate sum is debited and increases the value of the stock held by the business.

Returns outwards account

This is for the cost of goods returned by the business to its suppliers. The appropriate sum is credited and reduces the value of the stock held by the business.

There must be at least one stock account (possibly incorporating returns inwards and returns outwards) but many businesses have a number of them, perhaps even hundreds or thousands. This is to identify accurately the different categories of finished goods, and perhaps of raw materials, components and work in progress. Keeping different accounts may assist in stock control, stocktaking and the efficient management of the business. Some businesses have a stock purchases account for stock acquired and a stock sales account for stock sold. If this is done, the value of stock held by the business is the difference between the two, after adding the opening balance of course.

Shown below are illustrations of the double entry postings for different types of transactions involving stock.

Purchase of stock for cash

Goods costing £8,000 are purchased on 4 April. Stock (the asset account) is debited and cash (which is being diminished) is credited.

Stock Account

Debit		Credit
	£	£
4 April Cash Account	8,000	

Cash Account

Debit		Credit
	£	£
		4 April Stock Account 8,000

Purchase of stock on credit

Goods costing £5,000 are purchased on 6 April on credit from Dennis Clinton Ltd. Stock (the asset account) is debited and Dennis Clinton Ltd (a liability account) is credited. Dennis Clinton Ltd is a creditor because money is owed to it.

Stock Account

Debit		Credit
	£	£
6 April Dennis Clinton Ltd 5,000		

Dennis Clinton Ltd

Debit		Credit
	£	£
	6 April Stock Account 5,000	

Goods returned inwards for credit

Goods with a cost value of £1,000 that had been supplied to Hannah Smith Ltd are returned for credit on 7 April. Stock (the asset account) is debited and Hannah Smith Ltd is credited. This money is owing to Hannah Smith Ltd and it must be paid to her, or it may of course reduce the amount that Hannah Smith Ltd owes.

Returns Inwards Account

Debit		Credit
	£	£
7 April Hannah Smith Ltd 1,000		

Hannah Smith Ltd

Debit		Credit
	£	£
	7 April Returns Inwards	
	Account 1,000	

Goods returned outwards for credit

Goods that had been purchased for £2,000 are returned by the business to Cilla and Green (the supplier) on 8 April. Stock (the asset account) is credited and Cilla and Green is debited.

Returns Outwards Account

Debit		Credit
£		£
	8 April Cilla and Green	2,000

Cilla and Green

Debit		Credit
£		£
8 April Returns Outwards Account 2,000		

Sale of stock for cash

Goods that were purchased for £2,000 are sold on 3 May for £3,712. The asset of stock has been reduced and must therefore be credited with £2,000. The sale value of £3,712 is irrelevant for the stock account, though of course the necessary bookkeeping entries must be made elsewhere. The £2,000 must be debited to the profit and loss account, or trading account, which will reflect a profit of £1,712 on the sale. The entry to the profit and loss account may be confusing but it is explained in Chapter 7.

Stock Account

Debit		Credit
£		£
	3 May Profit and Loss Account	2,000

Profit and Loss Account

Debit			Credit
		£	£
3 May Stock Account	2,000		

Sale of stock on credit

Goods that were purchased for £4,000 are sold on credit to Litman Ltd on 5 May for £8,199. The asset of stock has been reduced and must therefore be credited with £4,000. The sale value of £8,199 is irrelevant for the stock account, though of course the necessary bookkeeping entries must be made elsewhere. The £4,000 must be debited to the profit and loss account or trading account, which will reflect a profit of £4,199 on the sale. The entry for the profit and loss account may be confusing but, again, it is explained in Chapter 7.

Stock Account

Debit			Credit
	£		£
		5 May Profit and Loss	
		Account	4,000

Profit and Loss Account

Debit			Credit
		£	£
5 May Stock Account	4,000		

The above is an outline of the bookkeeping entries but, other than in a very small and simple business, it is likely to get complicated. As stated earlier, there may well be many different accounts to record separately different categories of goods bought in for resale, and perhaps for different types of raw material, different categories of work in progress and different categories of manufactured goods. The sum of all these accounts will (or at least should) equal the total value of the stock held by the business.

In the dark ages, before computers and when top football players earned not much more than the people who paid to watch them, it was usual for manual stock cards or bin cards to be maintained, and it is just possible that you will come across them, though it is much more likely that a computerised system will do the same job, perhaps using different accounts in the nominal ledger and perhaps maintained outside the nominal ledger. Whatever the system it will book stock in and out and keep a running total of what is held. As well as needed for bookkeeping purposes this is needed for re-ordering and management control.

A modern computerised system is likely to be integrated into procedures geared for automatic re-ordering, payment of suppliers, raising sales invoices to customers and providing information to facilitate management control. Even the most modern system depends on the input of data and the sources of the data are likely to include:

Advice note

This is notification from a supplier that goods will be delivered in response to an order. It may be used as confirmation that an order has been processed.

Delivery note

This usually accompanies goods when they are delivered. It may be used to update the records or as the trigger for a goods received note made out by the receiving business. It may well have a part in the process of approving suppliers' invoices for payment, and auditors are likely to consider it important.

Stores requisition note

This is, as its name suggests, a request to issue goods from stock. It should, of course, be authorised in accordance with an agreed procedure.

Millions of words, to say nothing of accounting standards, have been written about the correct ways in which stock should be valued. It is a very big subject and this chapter only has room for just one of the principles. There is more about stock valuation and stocktaking in Chapter 6.

The first and most important principle is that stock should be held in the books at the lower of cost or net realisable value. This is almost universally accepted practice, though businesses in trouble may be tempted to cheat. This means that even if stock has genuinely increased in value, the increase should not be reflected in the accounts. The reason is hopefully obvious, namely it might never be sold. There is probably an empty shop somewhere near you where, sadly, the owner has had to close down and sell off the stock below cost price. It happens to large businesses too.

On the other hand, if the realisable value of an individual item or category of stock has fallen below the price that was paid for it, its value in the accounts should be reduced. This can happen for a number of reasons, changing fashion being an obvious example. Obsolescence is another possibility. Not all that many years ago a typical desktop calculator cost fifty times as much as today's models. Furthermore, it was fifty times the size and had only a fraction of the calculating capacity. It was a mistake to hold such stock for long without writing it down. I know because I was Financial Controller of a company that sold them.

It may also be necessary to write down the value of stock for other reasons. These can include theft, damage, loss, shrinkage and evaporation. A decision to write down the value of stock should be recorded in detail in a journal entry. The following is an example of such a journal with the consequent bookkeeping postings:

Journal

	Debit	Credit
	£	£
8 June Stock		2,000
JV163 Profit and Loss Account	2,000	

To reduce value of stock consequent upon the theft of 100 Smithson radios purchased for £20.00 each.

Stock Account

Debit			Credit
	£		£
		8 June JV163	2,000

Profit and Loss Account

Debit		Credit
	£	£
8 June JV163	2,000	

Value added tax

VAT is a simple concept that has somehow managed to get very complicated in practice. Its complexities once led to a celebrated court case to establish whether a jaffa cake is a cake or a biscuit. If you enjoy a jaffa cake with your afternoon tea, you will be pleased to know that you are eating a cake which is zero-rated, rather than a chocolate-covered biscuit which carries VAT at the standard rate. This is because it has the characteristics of a cake, especially in that it starts life soft and tends to get harder in time. A chocolate-covered biscuit, on the other hand, starts life hard and tends to get softer in time. It took the best legal brains in Britain a long time to establish that.

The subject of VAT is so large that this chapter only has room for a few key points. There is much more. What follows relates to the laws of the United Kingdom.

VAT is chargeable on transactions made in the UK when the goods or services are supplied 'in the course or furtherance of any business'. 'Business' is taken to encompass activity conducted in a business-like way, which means that some charities have to register for VAT and account for it on their business income. Supplies made outside the UK are outside the scope of UK VAT.

The concept is that every time a VAT-registered business makes a sale, VAT is added to the amount charged to the purchaser. The purchaser must pay this to the seller, but if it is a VAT-registered business the seller can recover it. Each VAT-registered business must periodically pay to HMRC the difference between VAT that it has charged (outputs) and VAT that it has paid (inputs). If the inputs are greater than the outputs, a payment to the business is made by HMRC. This continues up a chain provided that all the parties are VAT-registered businesses. It stops when a sale is made to a consumer or a business that is not VAT-registered. This person or business pays the VAT and has no way of recovering it. It is a bit like the children's game of pass the parcel. It is all good fun until the music stops. Features of VAT in the UK include:

Exempt supplies

Certain business supplies are exempt from VAT.

Zero-rated supplies

Zero-rated supplies are within the scope of VAT but the rate charged is nil. The supplier may recover its VAT inputs. Examples of zero-rated supplies are books and newspapers, exports, passenger transport and children's clothing. If a business makes only zero-rated supplies, it must tell Customs but, with their permission, need not register.

Reduced-rate supplies

VAT is charged on the supply of certain goods and services at the reduced rate, which at the time of writing is 5%. The supply of domestic fuel and power is an example of a reduced-rate supply.

Standard rate

If a supply is not zero-rated, subject to the reduced rate, exempt or treated as outside the scope of VAT (such as salaries), then it is standard-rated. At the time of writing the standard rate in the UK is 17.5%. VAT commenced in April 1973 with a standard rate of 10%. It was cut to 8% on 29 July 1974 and then raised to 15% on 18 June 1979. It was raised again to the present rate of 17.5% on 1 April 1991.

Registration

A business that only makes exempt supplies cannot register and cannot reclaim the VAT on its inputs.

A business that only makes zero-rated supplies must register and can reclaim the VAT on its inputs.

Other businesses that supply goods or services in a business capacity must register if their turnover is above the registration threshold. They may choose to do so (and recover their VAT inputs) if their turnover is below the registration threshold.

It is a legal requirement that, if requested to do so, a seller charging VAT must provide the purchaser with a proper VAT invoice that shows its VAT registration number. If this is not provided, the purchaser should not pay the VAT to the seller and must not reclaim it as a VAT input. The good news is that although the legal issues may be troublesome, the bookkeeping should be straightforward and probably will not cause any difficulties.

It is essential that there is a VAT account in the nominal ledger. Many businesses choose to have two, one for inputs and one for outputs, and some businesses have a more complicated structure of VAT accounts. The examples that follow assume that there is just one VAT account.

The bookkeeping system must be designed so that the VAT element of sales (outputs) is identified and posted to the VAT account. Similarly, the VAT element of purchases (inputs) is identified and posted to the VAT account. It follows that the balance of the VAT account is a running total of the amount owing to or from the Customs and Excise part of Her Majesty's Revenue and Customs (HMRC). As an example of what should be done, VAT columns should be incorporated in the cash book and the VAT element of purchases and sales should be posted to the VAT account. The following repeats the payments side of the cash book shown in Chapter 3. However, VAT at 17.5% has been charged on all items except the bank charges.

Amount	VAT	Stationery	Legal and professional	Bank charges
£	£	£	£	£
200.68	29.89		170.79	
33.11	4.93	28.18		
10.00	-			10.00
111.00	16.53		94.47	
44.00	6.55	37.45		
398.79	57.90	65.63	265.26	10.00

The following entries illustrate the postings. Claphorn and Crayfish Ltd makes a sale on credit of £10,000 to Dashwood and Dorkins Ltd on 3 May. VAT of £1,750 is added to the invoice making a total of £11,750. This appears in the books for Claphorn and Crayfish as follows.

Sales Account

Debit			Credit
	£		£
		3 May	10,000

VAT Account

Debit			Credit
	£		£
		3 May	1,750

Dashwood and Dorkins Ltd

Debit			Credit
		£	£
3 May	11,750		

The appropriate identifying posting reference must be shown. Hopefully you will remember from the second chapter that VAT is a liability account in the balance sheet, and that a credit balance indicates that money is owing.

Mirror postings will be made in the books of Dashwood and Dorkins Ltd with £1,750 posted as a debit to the VAT account. This sum may be deducted from the credits when the VAT return is completed and the payments to Customs and Excise is made.

Payroll and associated matters

Wages and salaries are very often grouped together and it is not easy to fix the distinctions between them. It is hard to believe that snobbery does not sometimes play a part. It is sometimes said that wages are paid weekly, whereas salaries are paid monthly, and it is sometimes said that wages are paid in cash, whereas salaries are paid by cheque or bank transfer. Some contend that salaries are paid for office or professional work. Be that as it may, the distinctions in Britain are fast disappearing, partly because fewer workers are paid in cash and more workers are paid monthly rather than weekly.

Whether it is a wage or a salary, a worker is very unlikely to receive the full amount of it. In the words of a nineteenth-century judge, 'the state will insert its shovel into his or her stores and extract what many consider to be a distressingly large sum'. Of course you may not agree with this robust viewpoint and many do not. It is a legal requirement that the process be properly managed and the necessary entries made into the bookkeeping system.

Until almost the middle of the last century taxpayers paid their income tax directly to the Inland Revenue and employers were not involved. In practice most of them paid no income tax at all because the thresholds were set so that a man or woman with children and earning the average wage had nothing to pay. This, needless to say, is no longer the case. Almost all employees do pay income tax, even those receiving a wide range of state benefits, and it is deducted at source by employers via the PAYE system, which is compulsory. National insurance is also collected in this way. National insurance is in theory a compulsory insurance scheme whereby workers are insured for certain eventualities and pay for their state pensions. In fact it is a misnomer because there is no separate fund and the state pays benefits out of current income. Let us hope that future governments and voters are willing to pay our pensions and benefits when we need them.

The detailed operation of payroll systems is beyond the scope of this chapter. It will probably be complicated and the complexity seems to increase year by year. Most businesses use computerised systems for their payroll, either their own or that of a bureau. The needs of businesses differ and all the necessary information must be made available. Income may be complicated as well as the deductions, and it is very important that the correct calculations be entered. Mistakes can lead to underpayments or overpayments, and the possibility of cheating should be kept in mind. Auditors will certainly consider this. Employees can usually be relied upon to draw attention to any underpayments, though overpayments may not always be pointed out. Bonuses, overtime, and piecework may be amongst the different types of income.

Features of PAYE include the following:

- HMRC will issue a tax code for each employee and the employer must use this in calculating the income tax deductions to be made each week or month. The tax codes are based on individual circumstances and are designed to deduct the correct amount of tax (including higher rate tax if applicable), so that the correct amount of tax has been deducted evenly throughout each tax year ending on 5 April. The tax code may be changed from time to time to correct mistakes, allow for underpayments or overpayments or because of changing circumstances.
- Employees' national insurance contributions must be deducted. These are calculated according to published rates and tables, and are not based on individual codes.
- Employers must pay national insurance contributions too. You may have heard of Lloyd George's catchphrase in 1909, *'ninepence for fourpence'*. It meant that each employee would get ninepence worth of benefits by paying fourpence, and with the employer paying the rest. Interestingly Lloyd George set the payment age for the state pension at 70. Employers' national insurance contributions are calculated according to different principles and are of course not deducted from pay.
- Other factors may best be summarised by listing the remaining boxes on the year-end P35 form that must be submitted to HMRC.
  - Statutory Sick Pay recovered
  - Statutory Maternity Pay recovered
  - NIC compensation on Statutory Maternity Pay
  - Statutory Paternity Pay recovered
  - NIC compensation on Statutory Paternity Pay
  - Statutory Adoption Pay recovered

- – NIC compensation on Statutory Adoption Pay
  - – Funding received from HMRC to pay SSP/SMP/SPP/SAP
  Things have moved a long way since Lloyd George's *'ninepence for fourpence'.*
- Each month by a prescribed date (unless other arrangements are in place) the business must make a payment to HMRC. This is for the net amount due for all deductions and transactions in the prescribed period.
- After each tax year ending on 5 April each business must submit to HMRC detailed forms for each employee (with a copy to the employee), and summarising its whole obligations and payments during the year. Any mistakes must be rectified, with a further payment if necessary.

There may be other deductions to make, including compulsory ones relating to the repayment of student loans and in respect of an attachment of earnings order issued by a county court. Other possibilities include the repayment of loans made by the business, the collection of trade union subscriptions, donations to a group charitable giving scheme and payments in connection with a staff share purchase scheme.

Now for the bookkeeping entries and, as you can imagine, there are a lot of possibilities. Features of the entries should include the following:

- Assuming that the payments are made to employees' bank accounts via the BACS system, payment of the wages and salaries will be by a single cheque payable to the bank. The other side of the posting will be to a suspense account which we will call here 'Wages Suspense Account'.
- The balance in Wages Suspense Account must be journalled out to the appropriate accounts. Money owing to HMRC for income tax and national insurance must be credited to appropriately named creditor accounts and so

must money owing to any other person or organisation. The debit entries are to the various cost centre departmental accounts. Employers' national insurance contributions must be incorporated into these entries.

- When HMRC (and perhaps others) are paid, the creditor accounts must be debited and Bank Account (or perhaps Cash Account) must be credited.

All of this is illustrated by the following example. When you study it, remember that your organisation might use slightly different names for the accounts.

Stage 1

Parkplatt Ltd pays the monthly salaries by BACS payments to employees' bank accounts. On 25 June it issues a single cheque for £89,124.65 in respect of payment of the June salaries. The entries are:

	Debit £	Credit £
Wages Suspense Account	89,124.65	
Bank Account		89,124.65

Stage 2

Entries are made to reflect the following:

- The gross amount payable to employees was £124,888.18.
- Income tax deducted was £18,296.11.

- Employees' national insurance deducted was £14,117.42.
- Amounts deducted for the repayment of staff loans totalled £1,400.00.
- An amount of £300.00 was deducted from an employee's pay under the authority of an attachment of earnings order issued by Bedford County Court.
- £1,650.00 was deducted under a payroll giving scheme in connection with the Royal Society for the Prevention of Cruelty to Animals (RSPCA).
- Employers' national insurance contributions (not reflected in the gross amount of £124,888.18) total £17,946.32.
- The total cost to Parkplatt Ltd (including employers' national insurance contributions) is charged to six departments as follows:
  - Production Department   £56,672.49
  - Finance Department   £19,234.18
  - Sales Department   £27,661.38
  - Transport Department   £6,141.63
  - Service Department   £31,202.24
  - Administration Department   £1,922.58

The following entries must be made in the bookkeeping system, perhaps by journal, but an integrated computerised payroll system would probably do it automatically.

	Debit £	Credit £
Wages Suspense Account		89,124.65
PAYE Owing Account		18,296.11
Employees' National Insurance Account		14,117.42
Staff Loans Account		1,400.00
Payments To Court Pending Account		300.00
RSPCA Account		1,650.00
Employer's National Insurance Account		17,946.32
Production Department Salaries Account	56,672.49	
Finance Department Salaries Account	19,234.18	
Sales Department Salaries Account	27,661.38	
Transport Department Salaries Account	6,141.63	
Service Department Salaries Account	31,202.24	
Administration Department Salaries Account	1,922.58	
	142,834.50	142,834.50

Stage 3

On 7 July a cheque for £50,359.85 is drawn payable to HMRC. This appears to be very public spirited because tax and national insurance deducted between 7 June and 6 July must be paid to HMRC by 19 July. However, it is not really an early payment because the finance director puts the cheque in her desk for ten days. The bookkeeping entries are:

	Debit £	Credit £
Bank Account		50,359.85
PAYE Owing Account	18,296.11	
Employees' National Insurance Account	14,117.42	
Employer's National Insurance Account	17,946.32	

Stage 4

On 25 July cheques for the attachment of earnings deduction and the RSPCA are drawn. The entries are:

	Debit	Credit
	£	£
Bank Account		300.00
Payments To Court Pending Account	300.00	
Bank Account		1,650.00
RSPCA Account	1,650.00	

The net effect of all this activity (assuming that there were no brought forward balances) has been:

- Six departmental salary accounts have been debited a total of £142,834.50. These accounts will eventually be debited to the profit and loss account.
- Nothing is owing to HMRC.
- Nothing is owing in respect of the attachment of earnings deduction or the payroll giving scheme.
- Staff loans due to the company have been reduced by £1,400.00.

The trial balance

There are two very good reasons for taking out a trial balance. First, it is one of the steps towards preparing the profit and loss account and the balance sheet, and this is explained in Chapter 6. Second, it is proof that, subject to certain exceptions described shortly, the books are in good order. It is good practice to take out a trial balance regularly, perhaps once a month, and it is virtually essential to do so when the accounts are prepared. This means that if a mistake has to be found, only a month's entries need be checked.

Please note particularly the phrase 'take out the trial balance'. The trial balance is not an account and it does not involve posting. It is the listing of all the balances in the ledger. You will remember that for every debit there must be a credit. It follows that the total of all the debit balances must equal the total of all the credit balances. If they do not do so, then a mistake has been made.

There are limitations to the proofs provided by a trial balance. It may balance and yet the following three types of error will not be disclosed.

1. **A compensating error:** This is two mistakes of the same amount, one increasing or decreasing the debits and one increasing or decreasing the credits.
2. **An error of principle:** This means the right amount posted to the wrong account.
3. **A transaction omitted altogether.**

The first two types of these errors may never be discovered. The third type may or may not eventually be discovered, depending on the nature of the transaction that has not been posted. A supplier demanding payment of an unrecorded invoice may, for example, lead to its discovery. All three types of error are nasty and mean that two accounts in the bookkeeping system are wrong.

A difference on the trial balance will disclose one of the following mistakes:

- A mistake in listing or adding the trial balance.
- A wrong addition on an account.
- A mistake in writing out the brought forward balances.
- One side of an entry not posted (double entry not complete).
- Posting of wrong amount.
- A missing ledger sheet.

You might find the cause of a trial balance difference by means of a random search. However, it is much better to conduct the search in a systematic manner. You *must* locate the cause of the difference if you do the following in a *systematic* way:

1. Check the listing of the balances within the trial balance.
2. Check the addition of the trial balance.
3. Check the listing of the opening balances. These are either the balances brought down or the balances at the time that the last trial balance was agreed.
4. Check the addition of each individual account within the trial balance. Check from the brought forward balances or the balances making up the last trial balance.
5. Tick each individual posting during the period under review. Every debit should have a matching credit and there should be no unticked entries at the end.

If done properly, this must find the difference.

If, which is of course likely, you have a computerised bookkeeping system, all of this may sound archaic. This is because the system will automatically ensure that the books balance and, in effect, maintain an up-to-date trial balance from day to day. Nevertheless, it is vital if manual records are kept and, in any case, it is as well to know the theory, especially the types of errors that will not be disclosed by a trial balance. As mentioned in the last chapter, some computer systems may accept unbalanced input and put the difference to a suspense account. If this happens, you have a balanced trial balance and also a problem, or at least a job to do.

Questions to test your understanding

1. The stock account of Brown and Keen Ltd had a debit balance of £99,000 on 1 July. The following events occurred in July.
   - On 4 July goods costing £14,000 were purchased for cash.
   - On 6 July goods costing £8,000 were purchased from Knight Ltd on credit.
   - On 8 July goods costing £6,000 were purchased from Knight Ltd on credit.
   - On 12 July goods with a stock value of £3,000 were sold for £4,200. It was a cash transaction.
   - On 16 July goods with a stock value of £2,100 were returned to Knight Ltd for credit.
   - On 17 July a fire destroyed the entire stock. Fortunately no one was hurt.

   Write up the accounts to show these events. There is no need to write out the journal. Goods destroyed in the fire should be written off to the profit and loss account.

2. A business only supplies zero-rated goods and each year its annual turnover is only about £3,000. May it choose to register for VAT and recover the VAT part of its purchases?

3. The VAT section of this chapter shows the entries in the books of Claphorn and Crayfish Ltd following a sale to Dashwood and Dorkins Ltd Show the resulting entries in the books of the purchaser (Dashwood and Dorkins Ltd).

4. Killington Ltd pays the monthly salaries by BACS transfers to employees' bank accounts. On 26 November it issues a single cheque for £61,216.13 in respect of the payment of the November salaries. This sum is calculated after making the following deductions from employees' gross pay:

- £15,123.45 for income tax.
- £9,678.32 for employees' national insurance contributions.
- £500.00 for the repayment of a staff loan.

Employers' national insurance contributions (not reflected in the gross amount of £86,517.90) total £10,996.42. There are just two cost centres: Production Department which takes a charge of £63,111.48 and Administration Department which takes the remainder of the cost. Show the bookkeeping entries for the cheque and the consequent postings.

5. What are the three types of error that will not be disclosed by a trial balance?

INSTANT TIP

The trial balance proves that the books balance but some types of mistake may still have been made.

05

How does using a computer make bookkeeping easier?

Most businesses except the very smallest use computerised bookkeeping in some form. Sage sells a range of products but is by no means the only company in the market. As an alternative to buying a standard package, a business may have the in-house expertise to write its own software or simply to use a spreadsheet such as Microsoft Excel. This chapter explains the principles of computerised bookkeeping, concentrating on Sage, QuickBooks and Excel. The topics covered are as follows:

- The advantages of computerised bookkeeping.
- How to match paper records to computer data.
- Some precautions.
- Inputting data.
- Production of reports.
- Bookkeeping with spreadsheets.

The advantages of computerised bookkeeping

Little more than a decade ago, most basic accountancy was carried out using pen, fifteen-column ledger and calculator. Arguably, trainee accountants learned the nuts and bolts of double entry far more effectively in those days by manually recording bank transactions, year-end journals such as depreciation and accruals, and opening balances, arriving at an extended trial balance which formed the basis of the final accounts. Software such as Auditman began to ease the final accounts preparation as the trial balance figures, having been produced manually, were entered and converted into a format in line with the requirements of the Companies Act and Accounting Standards, but not until the mid to late 1990s did it become economic to have a computer on every desk. As this began to happen, manual bookkeeping became for many people a relic of a distant era; though, as Thomas Hardy wrote in *The Mayor of Casterbridge*, 'as in all such cases of advance, the rugged picturesqueness of the old method disappeared with its inconveniences'.

Arithmetical errors, which often take hours to trace, should be eliminated by a good software package or a well-structured spreadsheet. A common feature of manual bookkeeping is that control accounts may not balance – for example, the total of individual debtors does not equal the sales ledger control account, or the VAT control account does not match the VAT return. This should not happen with computerised bookkeeping. Bank reconciliations should be quicker and easier on computer.

Information can be shared more easily and passed between employees, or between accountant and client, via e-mail or disk. Errors can in many cases be corrected without fuss, though this can create problems of its own (see later). In short, most of the advantages of computers in other spheres apply also to computerised bookkeeping.

How to match paper records to computer data

It is a common misconception that computerised bookkeeping inevitably does away with the need for paper. This may be the case if you have a reliable scanning system, but for most businesses the paperless office is as far away as ever. Every piece of data which is entered into the computer must be explainable in some way.

Bookkeeping entries will commonly fall into four categories: sales invoices, purchase invoices, bank transactions and non-cash journals.

The computer system should automatically number sales invoices in sequence, and indeed since 1 October 2007 sequential numbering has been a legal requirement for VAT-registered businesses. It is not strictly necessary to keep a paper copy of every sales invoice, provided that a copy can be reproduced from the system on demand, but it is good practice to keep a printout of the sales day book (see Chapter 2), and the auditors will invariably ask to see it.

Purchase invoices too should be sequentially numbered on receipt. This internal number is not to be confused with the supplier's invoice number. If the business does not operate a scanning system, they should be duly authorised and filed in numerical order so that they can be easily retrieved by the auditors or VAT inspectors. VAT-registered businesses should be aware that every item of VAT reclaimed on purchases must be backed up by a VAT invoice, and if the inspector cannot find one, he has the right to demand that the business pay the VAT back. Under VAT law, purchase invoices must be retained for six years (from the date of the invoice). It is acceptable to scan and then shred invoices provided that they can readily be converted into a legible form at the request of a VAT inspector.

Most bank payments and receipts relate to purchase and sales invoices, but there will be others which do not. They commonly relate to salaries, tax and direct debits. It is good practice to reference each such transaction in the computer system to a paper document such as an authorised payroll, a tax return or a direct debit instruction. The last category is the one which businesses most commonly forget to file in a logical order, which causes headaches for auditors.

Non-cash journals will typically include depreciation of fixed assets, adjustments to tax liabilities, loan interest, accruals and prepayments, and correction of errors. The temptation for a busy bookkeeper is to key these journals into the computer and make a mental note to produce a paper document later, which is then forgotten. It is important to create an audit trail at the time of posting, which may be in the following form:

	DR	CR
Electricity and gas		350.78
Stationery	350.78	

Correction of purchase ledger invoice 10045.

Date of posting: 15 January 2008
Accounting period: December 2007

Journal number: 2976

Some precautions

Software errors

Even freely available off-the-peg packages can contain errors. Some of them are updated once a year and it is wise to give a new package a few months to 'bed down' so that errors can be sorted out before the business purchases its own.

Many companies use their own custom-written software. This needs to be thoroughly tested before use. In one example seen by the author, the software indicated a gross profit some £100,000 lower than management expectations. It took several days to discover that a stock purchase had been correctly recorded in expenditure and creditors but the computer had not included it in the value of closing stock. Why this happened was a mystery, since all other similar transactions had been treated correctly, and it was put down to an error in the writing of the software.

A good software package will flash on the screen a warning whenever a journal is posted to the sales or purchase ledger control account. This is because the total of the individual ledger accounts may then not match the control account total.

The use of spreadsheets (see later in this chapter) for bookkeeping is very flexible and inexpensive. They are also more prone to errors than most software packages. A common error is to add an extra line to a list of items and not amend the formula which totals the list. To prevent formulae from being amended or additional rows and columns from being inserted in an Excel spreadsheet without authorisation, there is a useful feature which is operated as follows:

1. Select the cells on the worksheet that you *do* want the user to be able to amend (these should be the data input cells only), click on Cells/Format and untick the 'Locked' box.
2. Select Tools/Protection/Protect Sheet and enter a password.

If, for example, you wish the user to enter values in A1 to A10 with a sum total in A12, unlocking A1 to A10 will enable data to be entered in these cells but the 'sum' formula in A12 remains unalterable.

Authorisation

Entries into the computer system should be made only under appropriate passwords. This is especially sensitive with purchase ledger entries. Without adequate controls, an employee could post bogus purchase invoices and effect payment to an accomplice, or even fraudulently amend the bank account details of an existing supplier so that payment is diverted.

It is recommended that the system allows bank account details to be amended only under two passwords. As for purchase invoices, they could be entered in batches under one password and then 'locked' by a supervisor's password before being cleared for payment.

A daily printout of items entered into the computer could be scanned by a senior employee to ensure that no glaring errors have occurred. This might increase the possibility of catching an error such as one seen by the author in which expenditure was misdescribed and VAT of £14,000 was not reclaimed.

A good feature of some software packages is the automatic recognition of duplicate invoices. An invoice with the same number as one already entered into the system will be rejected.

Backup procedures

Computerised records may be more convenient but carry more risks. Computer breakdown can cause temporary lack of access and may even lead to the complete loss of data. The company which was recently sent five million e-mails by a single employee, suffering damage which cost £30,000 to put right, would no doubt concur.

It is good practice to retain daily printouts of items keyed into the computer. In addition, a series of backup disks should be made and at least one kept away from the site where the computers are located. There is little excuse for not doing this now that high capacity data sticks are available. This is common sense when one considers the possibility of fire or theft.

HMRC will sometimes waive penalties for late VAT Returns if the delay was caused by a computer breakdown, but only if the business took reasonable steps to prevent this happening.

Year-end journals

The final trial balance for an accounting year should exactly match the financial statements. Too often, auditors discover that this is not the case. Auditors examining the accounts for the year ended 31 December 2007, for example, will want to see that the retained profit brought forward at 1 January 2007 corresponds to that on the balance sheet at 31 December 2006.

Auditors will often hand the bookkeeper final journals at the end of an audit, usually for depreciation, accruals and prepayments. These should be entered into the computer and a final trial balance produced. If the business is satisfied that this reflects the figures in the final accounts, the year in question should be 'locked' so that no further entries can be mistakenly posted.

Confidentiality

Recent news items have highlighted the consequences of failure to guard computerised information with due care. Every business owes a duty of confidentiality to its employees, suppliers and customers, and if their details are held on computer, adequate precautions must be taken to avoid leakage.

Inputting data

Other than retailers who usually make a large volume of one-off sales, most businesses record their sales by customer. They may need to know the volume of sales made to a particular customer over a given period, especially if they grant bulk discounts, and a feature of a good credit control system is the ability to tell at a glance how much is owed by each customer, whether any amounts are overdue and whether a prompt payment discount should be allowed. The same applies in reverse to purchases. A good computerised bookkeeping system will, subject to correct and well-organised data input, provide all this information to a business and may even print invoices and statements.

Recording sales and purchases in Sage

You will now be taken through a sales transaction using Sage 50 Accounts (formerly known as Sage Line 50). The business, which provides accountancy services, is invoicing Snowdon Ltd for £2,000 plus VAT.

The starting point with Sage is to enter a new customer. Having entered the name of the customer (Snowdon), the user is asked for copious details including contact information, credit limit, settlement terms and bank account. Much of this can be left blank if deemed unimportant – this will vary from business to business. Sage asks for an account code which is important for reporting purposes, and consistency is the key here: many businesses use the first two letters of the customer's name followed by two numbers – in this case SN01.

A business with several classes of income may also wish to allocate each sale to a nominal code. This enables total sales to be analysed between classes of sale when the profit and loss account is produced. Sage comes with a large number of codes which are already numbered, and these can be seen by selecting 'Company', 'Reports', 'Nominal Details Reports', 'Nominal List' and 'Generate Report'. Broadly, the codes each consist of four digits and fall into the following categories:

Code starting	Category
0	Fixed assets
1	Current assets
2	Liabilities
3	Capital
4	Sales
5	Direct costs
6	Wages and salaries
7 and 8	Overheads
9	Drawings

In this case, the business may wish to rename the early '4' codes to reflect the various types of sale – perhaps 4000 could be 'Accountancy', 4001 'Audit' and 4002 'Taxation'. As well as assisting management with internal reporting, this has the added advantage of helping very large companies who in their annual financial statements must analyse sales between type and location. This is known as segmental reporting.

The business is now ready to enter the invoice. This is achieved via the 'Post invoices' screen. The format in this example needs to be changed to 'Services' (the default format is 'Products'), and then a description of the service and the amount (£2,000) should be entered. VAT at 17.5% (£350) is automatically calculated. To ensure that the invoice is posted to the correct sales nominal code, the business needs to select the 'Footer' tab and enter the code under 'Global'. The VAT rate can also be changed here if desired. In order to post the invoice, the business needs to select 'Save' and then 'Update'.

The first invoice has now been entered. To see the fruits of these labours, the business may want to see a list of its debtors, its balance sheet and its profit and loss account.

The list of debtors can be accessed from the 'Customer' screen using the 'Aged balances' link, from which it can be seen that customer SN01 owes £2,350 and this is a current debt. If the invoice has not been paid within 30 days, the amount will move to the next column.

The profit and loss account and balance sheet can be located from the 'Company' screen and the 'Financials' link. The profit and loss account shows total sales (and profit) of £2,000. The balance sheet shows debtors of £2,350 and a VAT liability of £350, giving net assets of £2,000.

The procedure to record a purchase is similar to that for sales but in reverse. Sage has the added advantage that it produces cheques.

Sage also produces VAT returns. A weakness often highlighted by users is that Sage allows only one date to be entered in respect of each transaction. This poses problems when an invoice bears two dates, being an invoice date and a tax point. They will be different where a supplier delivers goods and does not send an invoice until more than 14 days have passed. If, for example, an invoice dated 4 April is sent in respect of a delivery made on 15 March and both supplier and customer complete a VAT return to 31 March, the supplier must account for VAT on its March return, and the customer is entitled to reclaim it on its return for the same period.

The problem for the customer is that it can enter only one date. If it enters the invoice date of 4 April, Sage will not include the VAT reclaim on its March return. If, however, it enters the tax point of 15 March, the VAT return will be correct but the aged creditor report will show the debt as becoming overdue earlier than it actually is. (Suppliers and customers usually agree payment terms by reference to a certain number of days after the invoice date.) There is no easy solution except to carry out manual adjustments to the VAT return.

Transactions in services are relatively simple to record. Sage also has procedures to enable product sales and purchases to be entered and keep records of stock.

Recording sales and purchases in QuickBooks

You will now be taken through an entire purchase transaction using QuickBooks Simple Start. The business purchases office supplies for £500 plus VAT – a total of £587.50.

As with Sage, the starting point is to enter a new supplier. QuickBooks asks for less information than Sage, and no supplier code is requested. The next step is to enter the 'Write cheques' screen. Unlike Sage, QuickBooks does not operate on nominal codes and simply has a 'drop down' list of expenditure types. Having selected 'office supplies', the user needs to choose the appropriate VAT code, which in this case is 'S' (standard – 17.5%). When the amount of £500 is entered, a cheque is automatically filled out for £587.50.

QuickBooks produces a profit and loss account, which now shows expenditure of £500, and a balance sheet (accessible via the 'Reports' option), which shows a bank overdraft of £587.50 and VAT reclaimable of £87.50. It also produces a VAT return (VAT100) which reflects the VAT reclaim. Although the Simple Start version can produce an aged debtors analysis, albeit less detailed than that produced by Sage, there is no such analysis available for creditors.

Production of reports

Sage

Some features included in Sage 50 Accounts are:

- Comparison of budgeted figures to actuals.
- List of possible duplicate transactions.
- A VAT return which recognises sales and purchases to

and from traders in other countries within the European Union, which must be reported separately in Boxes 8 and 9 of the return.

- Online submission of VAT returns.
- Cash flow forecasting.
- Links to online banking.

Sage Line 100 has more extensive facilities to deal with credit control, stock control and job costing, and it provides in-depth financial reporting including the management of subsidiaries. Sage sell a range of more complex packages up to Sage 1000 which can be configured to meet the reporting requirements of other countries, has enhanced credit management features including the facility to log calls and cheque promises, assists with project and marketing management, and helps maximise resources for distribution by the timing of stock purchases and the allocation of drivers and vehicles.

Sage 50 Accounts is, however, adequate for the vast majority of businesses. Most small companies would find Sage 1000 well beyond their needs, understanding and budget.

QuickBooks

QuickBooks Simple Start is more straightforward (and cheaper) than Sage 50 Accounts for those who are new to bookkeeping. It relies more on words than codes, and the report screens are easier to find. It is, however, more limited in its scope.

QuickBooks Pro has additional features including stock tracking, but a business wishing to use its software to prepare a full trial balance will really need to consider QuickBooks Premier, which has advanced journaling features such as reversing journals (useful for accruals – see Chapter 6).

Cashcall

Cashcall, a product sold by Data Developments, is mentioned here specifically in the context of charity accounting. Whereas ordinary businesses simply have one line in their financial statements for retained profits, charities have to allocate their surpluses and deficits either to the 'general fund' or to one of a number of 'designated funds' (money allocated by the trustees for a particular purpose) or 'restricted funds' (money donated for a specific purpose). Many software packages do not deal adequately with this and automatically post all surpluses and deficits to the general fund. The charity then has to post a complicated series of journals to move the entries to another fund.

Cashcall has been designed specifically for fund accounting. It deals with year-end journals such as accruals and prepayments and produces a set of financial statements which comply with charity law.

Bookkeeping with spreadsheets

Spreadsheet bookkeeping is usually suitable only for small, simple businesses; but with the cost of a standard software package usually exceeding £300, spreadsheets are often worth the time spent in designing them and the added flexibility. This section will demonstrate how to analyse bank transactions using Microsoft Excel.

Bank transactions

In the following example, a business with an opening bank balance of £8,657.33 has four bank payments and three bank receipts as follows:

	£
Payments	
Goods for resale	1,000.00
Salaries	3,000.00
Rates	344.50
Goods for resale	500.00
Receipts	
Sales	4,500.00
Interest	45.00
Sales	2,000.00

It designs a spreadsheet with three worksheets: bank payments, bank receipts and bank summary.

The bank payments sheet is set out as follows:

Microsoft Excel - Bank transactions.xls

File   Edit   View   Insert   Format   Tools   Sage   Data   Window   Help

Arial   11   B   I   U

C5   fx =IF($B5=C$2,$A5,0)

	A	B	C	D	E	F
1						
2			1	2	3	
3	Amount		Goods for resale	Rates	Salaries	
4						
5	1,000.00	1	1,000.00	-	-	
6	3,000.00	3	-	-	3,000.00	
7	344.50	2	-	344.50	-	
8	500.00	1	500.00	-	-	
9						
10	4,844.50		1,500.00	344.50	3,000.00	
11						

Cell C5 contains a formula which is copied to all the other cells in the range C5 to E8:

$$=IF(\$B5=C\$2,\$A5,0)$$

The effect of this is that the number entered in column B dictates the column (C, D or E) into which the expenditure is analysed. The formula is saying, 'If B5 is the same figure as C2, I will copy A5 to C5; if not, I will enter zero.'

The '$' sign in a formula is a useful feature when copying and pasting the formula to other cells. To give a simple example, if cell J6 contained the formula:

$$=J3+J4$$

and this was copied and pasted to L10, the formula in L10 would normally read:

$$=L7+L8$$

If, however, J6 contained the formula:

$$=J\$3+J\$4$$

and this was copied and pasted to L10, column J would change but rows 3 and 4 would not, resulting in:

$$=L\$3+L\$4$$

The bank receipts sheet is set out as follows and on the same principles:

	A	B	C	D	E	F
			fx =IF($B5=C$2,$A5,0)			
1						
2			1	2		
3	Amount		Sales	Interest		
4						
5	4,500.00	1	4,500.00	-		
6	45.00	2	-	45.00		
7	2,000.00	1	2,000.00	-		
8						
9	6,545.00		6,500.00	45.00		
10						

Microsoft Excel - Bank transactions.xls — cell C5 selected, formula bar: =IF($B5=C$2,$A5,0)

Finally, the bank summary sheet would look like this:

	A	B	C
		fx =SUM(B1:B5)	
1	Balance brought forward	8,657.33	
2			
3	Receipts	6,545.00	
4	Payments	-4,844.50	
5			
6	Balance carried forward	10,357.83	
7			

Microsoft Excel - Bank transactions.xls — cell B6 selected, formula bar: =SUM(B1:B5)

The receipts and payments totals are taken from formulae linked to the respective worksheets.

Other information

The information gathered from the bank transactions could feed into an extended trial balance which is the basis for the final accounts. This is discussed in Chapter 6.

Spreadsheets could also include a summary of VAT transactions, accruals and prepayments, tax computations, schedules of fixed assets, and information to be included in the statutory financial statements such as an analysis of loans and lease agreements, staff costs and segmental analysis. They may assist with ratio analysis, which is important not only for applications for bank borrowing but also for the directors' report, which for larger companies must now give details of 'key performance indicators'. These may include the ratios discussed in Chapter 10; if the financial statements are compiled on a spreadsheet, the ratios oan automatically be calculated and updated. Graphs are also a useful feature of most spreadsheets, though the skills needed to compile them are quite advanced. Formulae and figures can also be copied across different worksheets. To get full benefit from using spreadsheets, it would be advisable to take a short course, or read a book such as *Teach Yourself Excel 2007* by Moira Stephen.

Questions to test your understanding

1. Why might the following journal entry be automatically questioned by a good computerised bookkeeping package?

DR VAT control account	30.60
CR Sales ledger control account	30.60

2. Which numbers in Sage would you expect the following nominal accounts to begin with?
   a) Plant and machinery
   b) Bank loans
   c) Loans to employees
   d) Cost of raw materials
   e) Pension contributions made by company for employees
3. If VAT code 'S' were selected in Sage, how much VAT would be added to an invoice for £3,000?
4. Which one of the following will an Excel spreadsheet not normally do?
   a) Round figures to the nearest whole number.
   b) Find the cells which are affected if a number is entered in a particular cell.
   c) Link to Revenue and Customs' website and automatically update for changes in tax law.
   d) Calculate the number of days between two dates.

INSTANT TIP

When entering an item into the computer, it is easy to get everything else right and then post the item into the wrong accounting period. This will make not only this year's accounts wrong, but also last year's accounts.

06

What preparations are necessary for producing the accounts?

So far in this book we have studied various aspects of bookkeeping and some associated matters. At the end of Chapter 4 the trial balance was explained, this being of course the listing of all the accounts and balances in the ledger. If the business was extremely simple and small, if the accountants were good and if the accounts did not have to be prepared quickly, it might be possible to prepare the profit and loss account and balance sheet by just extracting the appropriate balances.

In practice it is unlikely to be that simple. An extremely good start is to do the bank reconciliation and other reconciliations as appropriate. If there is a suspense account, and there probably is, it should be investigated and its constituent parts journalled out where this can be done. If possible the various entries should be posted whilst the books are still open. If this cannot be done, the entries should be done as part of the adjustments.

There are almost always three sets of adjustments to be made and they are studied in this chapter. They are:

- Depreciation and fixed assets.
- Accruals and prepayments.
- Reserves and provisions.

There may be other types of adjustment as well.

The chapter continues with an explanation of how the final adjustments are posted and the extended trial balance.

Taking an unduly harsh or lenient view of the accruals and provisions is a relatively common way of influencing the profit or loss for a particular year. A purist (and I am something of a purist) will say that affecting the profit in this way should not be done. At one end of the scale it is criminal deception and at the other it may be seen as no more than reasonable prudence. There may be a variety of motives. Holding down the profit is a way of delaying (but not avoiding) tax. There is an obvious incentive if tax rates are to be cut in the following year. Managers may have an incentive to boost the profit if their bonuses depend on it.

Manipulating the profit in this way may succeed in the short term, but it does not work in the long term. This is because all the adjustments are reversed in the next period, and if you have declared too much profit, you have to do extra well in the next period in order to catch up. For obvious reasons it is safer to understate the profit rather than overstate it, but both are wrong.

Depreciation and fixed assets

Fixed assets must be differentiated from current assets and investment assets. Current assets are assets with a value available to the business in the short term, which is usually taken to mean up to a year. These are cash and assets used in the course of business, such as stock and debtors (money owing by customers). Investment assets are held as an investment rather than for use in the business, such as shares.

Fixed assets are assets expected to realise value to the business in the long term, which is usually taken to mean more than a year. Examples are motor vehicles, plant and machinery, fixtures and fittings, computers, freehold property and leasehold property.

Before depreciating a fixed asset, it is as well to confirm that it still exists. Usually the answer is a readily ascertainable yes, but it is as well to check. If the asset has been destroyed or lost, it should be written off rather than depreciated, and if it has been sold, the correct bookkeeping entries should have been made.

We need to depreciate fixed assets because in almost all cases they will lose value over time. The reasons for this include:

Wear and tear

Assets wear out with use. Your old car with 100,000 miles on the clock is less valuable than when it was new. Furthermore, assets may be subject to rust, rot etc. even if not used.

Obsolescence

Some assets lose value through obsolescence, even if working perfectly and with every prospect of a long working life ahead. Computers are an obvious example.

Depletion

A quarry is the classic example. A quarry that once contained 100,000 tons of aggregates is not as valuable when some of the aggregates have been extracted.

The passage of time

A lease is an excellent example. A leasehold property with a ten-year lease is not worth as much when part of the ten years has elapsed.

What would happen if fixed assets were not depreciated? The answer is that the accounts would be inaccurate. The balance sheet would overstate both the value of the fixed assets and the net worth of the business. The profit and loss account would overstate the profit or understate the loss. This would continue each year (to a greater and greater extent in the case of the balance sheet) until the asset was finally sold or scrapped. At this point the balance sheet would be correct but the charge to the profit and loss account in the final year would be too much. It would be right in the long run but as the famous economist Maynard Keynes once remarked, *'In the long run we are all dead'*. The short term must be right too.

The bookkeeping entries to post depreciation are straightforward. The bookkeeping system will have an account 'Depreciation on ...' for each class of fixed asset. There will also be a Depreciation Account classed as an expense item. The following is the entry to record a depreciation charge of 25% on Plant and Machinery in the books at £10,000.

	Debit £	Credit £
Depreciation on Plant and Machinery		2,500
Depreciation	2,500	

After the entry has been passed the balance of the three accounts will be:

	Debit £	Credit £
Plant and Machinery	10,000	
Depreciation on Plant and Machinery		2,500
Depreciation	2,500	

The depreciation account balance of £2,500 will be debited to the profit and loss account, and will reduce the profit or increase the loss. Plant and Machinery will be valued in the balance sheet at £7,500 (£10,000 less £2,500).

If at this stage the Plant and Machinery is sold for £7,700 cash, the bookkeeping entries will be:

	Debit £	Credit £
Plant and Machinery		10,000
Depreciation on Plant and Machinery	2,500	
Cash	7,700	
Profit on Sale of Fixed Assets		200

The balance of £200 in the Profit on Sale of Fixed Assets account will be a credit to the profit and loss account, and will increase the profit or reduce the loss. There will be £7,700 in the bank and the Plant and Machinery will no longer appear in the balance sheet.

Certain businesses have specialised methods of calculating depreciation to meet their particular circumstances, but there are two main methods:

Straight line method

This has the advantage of simplicity and it is the most commonly used method. The original cost is written off evenly over a fixed number of years. So if an asset cost £10,000 and it is written off at 25% per year, £2,500 will be written off in each of four years. At the end of four years if the asset is still owned, it will be in the books at nil value.

This method is obviously the right one for an asset such as a lease. It may be a bit rough and ready but quite adequate for a range of other assets.

Reducing balance method

This method depreciates a fixed percentage of the written down value at the beginning of each year. It follows that the amount written off reduces each year, and that the written down value never reaches nil. This is probably realistic because, after all, even a 20-year-old car has some value.

An example of this is an item of machinery purchased for £100,000 and written off at 25% per year on the reducing balance method. The depreciation charge will be as follows:

Year 1	25% × £100,000	=	£25,000
Year 2	25% × £75,000	=	£18,750
Year 3	25% × £56,250	=	£14,063

Accruals and prepayments

Accruals are made for the costs of goods and services, where the benefit has been received but the charge has not yet been entered in the books. It could for example be for the cost of some components that have been included in stock despite the supplier's invoice not having been received. Furthermore, suppliers' invoices may be lost or held up pending approval. The more quickly the books are closed off at the end of the accounting period, the more numerous will be the invoices not entered.

These problems can be overcome by entering what are called accruals. These are calculated in one of two ways:

1. A specific invoice received after the close off. If the electricity bill to 31 March is £1,507.46 and the accounts are done for the year to 31 March, then you will accrue £1,507. It would be most unusual to bother with the pence.

2. An informed estimate. If the electricity bill averages £1,000 a quarter, and the last bill is up to 15 March, it would be reasonable to accrue £170 at 31 March. It is usual for most accruals to be informed estimates.

The accounting entry is to debit the account of the expense (e.g. electricity) and to credit the accruals account. The accruals account is a liability account because it is money owing by the business. The bookkeeping entries are explained further at the end of this section.

Prepayments

If you understand accruals you will have no difficulty with prepayments, which are a mirror image of accruals. A prepayment is an accounting entry that adjusts for a cost that has been taken in advance.

A prepayment may be necessary because a supplier has raised an invoice early, or because you have left the books open to catch as many invoices as possible and one from the next period has slipped through. For example an invoice dated 3 July may slip through if you make the accounts up to 30 June, but leave the books open for two weeks beyond that date.

More usually, a prepayment may be necessary because an invoice has been entered that covers a benefit to be received in the future. A very common example is insurance which may be paid a year in advance.

We will consider an insurance invoice for £12,000 that has been paid on 31 December, and which pays for insurance cover over the following 12 months. Let us assume that the business prepared its accounts at 30 June. Obviously, unless an adjustment is made, overheads will be too large and the profit will be too small.

The answer is to prepay six twelfths of £12,000 which equals £6,000. Insurance (an overhead account) is credited with £6,000 and the prepayments account is debited £6,000. The prepayments account is an asset account because it represents money paid in advance for goods and services. It is like the deposit that you may pay in February for your summer holiday to be taken in August.

The following are the bookkeeping entries for the £170 electricity accrual and the £6,000 insurance prepayment mentioned above.

	Debit £	Credit £
Electricity	170	
Accruals		170
Insurance		6,000
Prepayments	6,000	

Electricity and Insurance are both accounts that will be transferred to the profit and loss account and will affect the profit. Accruals is money owing by the business and will be shown as a liability in the balance sheet. Prepayments represents money paid in advance and the business is entitled to receive goods or services or a refund. It is therefore shown as an asset in the balance sheet.

Accruals and prepayments are calculated when the profit and loss account and balance sheet are prepared. They are posted (or at least brought into the figures) in one period, then the entries must be reversed in the next period. Reversing the entries means that the accruals and prepayments accounts will revert to a nil balance. The profit and loss type accounts will show the correct charge in the following period. Consider the electricity account in the following period:

	Debit £	Credit £
Reversal of accrual		170
Electricity invoice	1,000	

The net effect would be a charge of £830 in the second period, which would be correct. This assumes that the electricity bill was exactly £1,000, which was the amount of the estimate. In practice, unless you are a clairvoyant, the actual amount would be different, but no one is perfect and hopefully the difference would be small.

Reserves and provisions

What is the difference between a reserve and a provision? I think that I knew once but, if I did, I have forgotten. Hardly anyone else knows either, which probably does not matter because the two terms are virtually interchangeable. It is so obscure that it reminds one of the former British Prime Minister Lord Palmerston's comment on the Schleswig Holstein question. He said that only three people had ever fully understood the Schleswig Holstein question. One was the Prince Consort, who was dead. A second was a Danish statesman, who was in an asylum. He, Palmerston, was the third, but he had forgotten. Unlike the difference between reserves and provisions, it did matter because in 1866 it led to a war between Prussia and Denmark. Despite there being no practical difference, books on accounting always refer to 'reserves and provisions'.

Reserves and provisions are made to cover events that may happen (or have actually happened) but are not adequately recorded in the books.

A bad debt reserve is an easily understood example. Company A made a credit sale of £100,000 to Company B. The entries in the books of Company A were:

	Debit £	Credit £
Sales account	100,000	
Trade debtors account		100,000

Good news so far. The balance of the sales account will eventually be credited to the profit and loss account and will increase profit. It is expected that Company B will soon send a cheque for £100,000 to clear the trade debtors account. But Company B's chairman is arrested and charged with fraud, the directors resign, the company goes into liquidation and the liquidator forecasts an eventual dividend of ten pence in the pound to unsecured creditors.

To put it mildly, the books of Company A do not reflect the true position. They overstate the true profit by £90,000. Company A will need the following entry in its books:

Bad debt reserve account	£90,000 credit
Bad debt account	£90,000 debit

The bad debt account is a charge to the profit and loss account. This reduces the £100,000 sale contribution to a realistic £10,000. The bad debt reserve account is placed against trade debtors account in the balance sheet. It is thus reduced to £10,000 which is the amount expected to be eventually paid.

Bad debt reserves may be against specific debts as above, or they may be a realistic general reserve. A major book club sells books to the public by post and sends out the books before payment is made. At any one time it is owed money by many thousands of different customers. Each debt is individually small. Experience may show that a bad debt reserve of say 5% of the total amount outstanding is necessary.

Reserves and provisions are necessary for more than just bad debts. The list is very long and you may well be able to think of some circumstances that relate to a business with which you are familiar. The following are just some of the possibilities:

- Provision for settlement discounts payable. Suppose that your business offers 5% settlement discount to all customers who pay within 30 days of invoice date. Unless you make a provision you will overstate the profits. Not all customers will take advantage of the settlement discount so perhaps a provision of 4% of the total sum outstanding would be realistic.
- Provision for fulfilling warranty claim obligations. Suppose that you supply double-glazed windows and guarantee to repair faulty workmanship free of charge for up to ten years after installation. A realistic provision for the cost of future repairs would be necessary.

- Provision for settlement of outstanding legal claims. These could be for alleged negligence, faulty workmanship, wrongful dismissal, libel, or many other matters. Again, a realistic estimate of the eventual cost should be provided.
- Provision for losses on a contract or joint venture. Perhaps one of these has gone wrong. Your organisation has a legal obligation to complete the work, but it is clear that at the end a loss will be made. Provision should be made for the loss as soon as it can realistically be foreseen. You should not wait to charge the profit and loss account in future years.

The bookkeeping entries follow the same principles as those for accruals and prepayments. A suitably named reserve or provision account should be set up. As an example, the following would be set up for the anticipated £90,000 bad debt mentioned earlier.

	Debit £	Credit £
Reserve for Bad Debts		90,000
Bad Debts Written Off	90,000	

The £90,000 in 'Bad Debts Written Off' would be transferred to the profit and loss account, and would decrease the profit or increase the loss. The £90,000 in 'Reserve for Bad Debts' would be set against debtors in the balance sheet and would reduce the amount owing to the business. Despite this the company could and should try to get payment of the complete £100,000. Time (perhaps a long time) would indicate whether the £90,000 reserve was too optimistic or too pessimistic. Suppose that a cheque for £9,802 is received later and that the prospects of a further receipt were then nil. The entries in a subsequent period would be:

	Debit	Credit
	£	£
Bank Account	9,802	
Bad Debts Written Off	198	
Debtors (named customer account)		100,000
Reserve for Bad Debts	90,000	

The £90,000 was too optimistic and the above entries transfer a further charge of £198 to the debit of the profit and loss account. These entries and the preceding one have removed the debt and the reserve from the balance sheet.

Posting the adjustments and the extended trial balance

It is usually necessary to list the trial balance, open the accounts for the next period, then work through a list of adjustments to the trial balance. There are nearly always accruals and prepayments. There are often reserves and provisions to enter, mistakes to be corrected, and there may be many other adjustments as well.

There are two approaches for posting the adjustments which we will consider in turn:

Actually posting the entries

All the adjustments are posted in the ledgers and then a new trial balance is listed. This new trial balance is used to prepare the accounts. All the adjustment entries are then reverse posted into the ledgers in the next period. This reverse posting is necessary because the ledgers have to be restored to the position before the adjustments.

This may be difficult to understand but consider an accrual of £1,000 for a late telephone bill. The accrual is a debit to the overhead account. In the next period the reverse posting puts a credit of £1,000 into the overhead account. When the actual invoice for £1,000 arrives it is a debit and cancels out the credit leaving a nil balance. This is correct because it was a late invoice which should affect only profit in the earlier period.

Computerised accounting systems usually operate in this way. This is because it is relatively simple for the computer to be programmed to reverse post automatically into the following period.

The extended trial balance

The second approach is to list all the adjustments into extra columns to the trial balance (one debit column and one credit column). The trial balance is then repeated taking account of the adjustments. The whole thing is on one piece of paper and there are six columns in total (sometimes eight columns but we will not bother with this). It is extremely important that all the adjustments are properly cross-referenced to a full list of the changes and a narrative explanation of them.

We will conclude by looking at an extended trial balance sheet for Bridget Murphy who is a public relations consultant. She commences business on 1 July and the extended trial balance is at the end of her first year in business on the following 30 June.

The extended trial balance is given and you should study it carefully. It incorporates adjustments to reflect the following:

- Motor vehicle and office equipment should both be depreciated by 25%.
- Bridget has not yet entered an invoice for £5,000 for work that she has done.
- Bank interest to 30 June not yet entered into the books is £2,643.
- On 30 June Bridget paid £2,400 insurance to cover a year in advance.
- Bridget has received invoices as follows but not entered them into the books:

Office expenses	£1,800
Travel expenses	£246
Stationery	£679

- Her telephone account averages £1,800 a quarter and she has paid the bill up to 31 May.
- Bridget believes that £1,000 owing to her will turn out to be a bad debt.

	Closing trial balance		Adjustments		Adjusted trial balance	
	Debit £	Credit £	Debit £	Credit £	Debit £	Credit £
Motor vehicles	20,000.00				20,000.00	
Office equipment	15,000.00				15,000.00	
Depreciation of motor vehicle				5,000.00		5,000.00
Depreciation of office equipment				3,750.00		3,750.00
Bank account		23,185.16				23,185.16
Trade debtors	5,708.31		5,000.00		10,708.31	
Trade creditors		661.19				661.19
Reserve for bad debts				1,000.00		1,000.00
Accruals				5,968.00		5,968.00
Prepayments			2,400.00		2,400.00	
Fees invoiced		64,000.00		5,000.00		69,000.00
Salaries	12,000.00				12,000.00	
Insurance	4,600.00			2,400.00	2,200.00	
Office expenses	7,309.14		1,800.00		9,109.14	
Travel expenses	11,111.18		246.00		11,357.18	
Stationery	3,209.47		679.00		3,888.47	
Telephone	6,908.25		600.00		7,508.25	
Interest	2,000.00		2,643.00		4,643.00	
Bad debts			1,000.00		1,000.00	
Depreciation			8,750.00		8,750.00	
	87,846.35	87,846.35	23,118.00	23,118.00	108,564.35	108,564.35

Questions to test your understanding

1. A new car is purchased for £16,000. What will be its written-down value after two years if it is:
   a) Depreciated at 25% per year using the straight line method?
   b) Depreciated at 25% per year using the reducing balance method?

2. Calculate and list the accruals and prepayments for a local authority staff restaurant that prepares accounts for a period ending on 31 May. The following information is available:
   - £70 invoice for bread from the wholesalers delivered on 8 June has been entered into the books before they were closed off.
   - The telephone account for the quarter to 31 March was £600. No later invoice has been received.
   - Six months' water rates in advance totalling £900 were paid on 31 March.
   - Food with a total value of £700 was delivered to the canteen on 29 May. No invoice has been received.
   - Wages average £350 a week and are paid weekly in arrears. Payment has been made for work done up to 26 May (a seven-day week is worked).

3. A business is owed £600,000 at the balance sheet date and customers are entitled to deduct 5% for prompt payment. In the past about half the customers have paid promptly and deducted the discount.
   a) Write the journal setting up the reserve.
   b) Write the journal for the following year when £592,000 has been received and £8,000 discount has been deducted.

INSTANT TIP

Taking an unduly harsh or lenient view of accruals and prepayments, or reserves and provisions, is a way of manipulating the profit figure. It does not work in the long term and It Is best to resist the temptation.

What exactly is a profit and loss account?

This book is about bookkeeping and accounting and the opening chapters were about bookkeeping, with Chapter 6 being a lead-in to the preparation of the accounts. The layman usually thinks first of the profit and loss account when accounts are mentioned, and that is the subject of this chapter. Published accounts are considered in Chapter 9, but this chapter concentrates on the basic principles of a profit and loss account, perhaps prepared for management purposes. The topics covered are:

- What is a profit and loss account?
- A straightforward profit and loss account.
- A trading business.
- A manufacturing business.
- Taxation and appropriation.

What is a profit and loss account?

A profit and loss account is a summary of all the revenue earned and expenses incurred in a specified period of time. It is a logical listing of all the accounts of an income and expense nature in the trial balance, with accounts representing assets, liabilities and capital being ignored. It should be properly headed and the period of time should be stated.

The chosen duration is often a year, especially in the case of published accounts, but other periods may be encountered. Internal profit statements prepared for management may be done weekly, monthly, quarterly or for some other convenient period. The steps in preparing the profit and loss account are:

1. Make sure that everything is posted up to date.
2. Post all the final adjustments. (This was explained in Chapter 6.)
3. List the final adjusted trial balance.
4. Extract the revenue and expense accounts and list them in a logical format. If the credit balances add to a sum greater than the debit balances, a profit has been made. If this is not the case, a loss has been made, though an excessively pedantic person might point to the exceedingly unlikely possibility of an exact break-even. The remaining accounts in the trial balance, plus the profit or loss, will form the basis of the balance sheet. (This is explained in Chapter 8.)
5. Open the ledger for the next period. The opening balances for the assets, liabilities and capital accounts will be the closing balances from the previous period. All the income and expense accounts will be opened with a nil balance. The net profit or loss will be transferred to the capital accounts, thus increasing or decreasing the amount of

capital that the owners have invested in the business. This ensures that the trial balance continues to balance.

6. The accruals and prepayments are reverse posted into the new period.

A straightforward profit and loss account

This example is about as simple as it gets. Sally Blanchflower starts business as a literary agent on 1 October. After posting the closing adjustments her trial balance at the following 31 March is:

	Debit £	Credit £
Accruals		806
Bad debts written off	300	
Bank account		9,035
Charitable donations	200	
Depreciation	1,050	
Depreciation on fixtures and fittings		50
Depreciation on motor vehicles		1,000
Electricity	317	
Entertaining	2,424	
Fees invoiced		27,900
Fixtures and fittings	1,000	
Hotel expenses	3,109	
Insurance	950	
Interest	1,123	
Motor vehicle	8,000	
Office expenses	4,761	
Postage	830	

Prepayments	600	
Rent	3,000	
Subsistence	2,617	
Telephone	720	
Travel expenses	1,400	
Trade creditors		1,716
Trade debtors	8,106	
	40,507	40,507

Accounts representing assets and liabilities should be ignored, and this includes 'Depreciation on fixtures and fittings' and 'Depreciation on motor vehicles'. The expense accounts and the one income account should be extracted and the profit and loss account is as follows.

Sally Blanchflower
Profit and loss account for the six months to 31 March

	£	£
Fees invoiced		27,900
Less expenses:		
Bad debts written off	300	
Charitable donations	200	
Depreciation	1,050	
Electricity	317	
Entertaining	2,424	
Hotel expenses	3,109	
Insurance	950	
Interest	1,123	
Office expenses	4,761	
Postage	830	
Rent	3,000	
Subsistence	2,617	
Telephone	720	
Travel expenses	1,400	
		22,801
Net profit		5,099

This will not reveal any arithmetical errors in writing down and adding the profit and loss account. However, the net profit will be transferred to the balance sheet, and if this does not balance the existence of a problem will be apparent. An error of principle, such as an asset account being listed as an expense in the profit and loss account, will not be revealed, so you have to be careful.

A trading business

A trading business is one that buys and sells goods. This definition encompasses wholesalers and retailers who sell goods (as opposed to shops that provide services, such as hairdressers). A manufacturing business sells goods that it has manufactured and this is considered later in this chapter.

It used to be common for a trading account to be prepared separately from the profit and loss account. This is still sometimes done, but you are more likely to see a combined trading and profit and loss account. It may just be called the profit and loss account. The trading account (or the trading part of the profit and loss account) is intended to establish the gross profit as a separate total before other costs are deducted. The gross profit is sales minus cost of sales. Cost of sales is opening stock plus stock purchases, less closing stock.

It should be obvious that the trading account must only show the cost of the goods sold in the period. This means sales where the revenue was recognised in the period in question. A wrong figure, perhaps a ridiculously wrong figure, will be obtained if the cost of goods purchased in the period is used.

The value of stock at the beginning and end of the period may be established by stocktaking, and the opening stock (the stock at the beginning of the period) should be the figure in the trial balance.

If financial controls are extremely good they may be calculated figures, with periodic stock checks to prove the system. If there has been any theft or other form of stock shrinkage, stock will be reduced and consequently the cost of sales will be increased. The principle is illustrated by the profit and loss account of a school tuck shop. There are no costs other than the cost of the food sold. The profit and loss account is given below.

Sales in the month of February total £430. Stock at 31 January was £100. Stock at 28 February was £120. Purchases in February were £380.

School Tuck Shop
Profit and Loss Account for February

	£	£
Sales		430
Stock at 31 January	100	
Add purchases in February	380	
	480	
Less stock at 28 February	120	
		360
Net profit		70

In this extremely simple example the gross profit is the same as the net profit. This is because there are no further costs.

The same principles apply in the profit and loss accounts of Tesco and Marks and Spencer, though of course the figures are very considerably bigger. These companies buy food and other products from their suppliers, they have stock checks at the beginning and end of each trading period (or they calculate the stock), and they sell to the public.

The following is an example of a trading and profit and loss account. It is still a simple example but there are costs to be brought in below the gross profit.

The trial balance of Scunthorpe Retail Gas Appliances Ltd at 31 May includes the following.

	Debit £	Credit £
Miscellaneous expenses	18,994	
Property costs	20,818	
Purchases	43,316	
Salaries	42,296	
Sales		128,126
Opening stock	47,631	
Transport	4,988	

The trading period covers two months and the stock figure of £47,361 was the figure established at a stocktake taken on 31 March. Stock at 31 May is £45,772. The profit and loss account is as follows.

Scunthorpe Retail Gas Appliances Ltd
Trading and Profit and Loss Account for the
two months to 31 May

	£	£
Sales		128,126
Stock at 31 March	47,631	
Add purchases	43,316	
	90,947	
Less stock at 31 May	45,772	
		45,175
Gross profit		82,951
Less:		
Miscellaneous expenses	18,994	
Property costs	20,818	
Salaries	42,296	
Transport	4,988	
		87,096
Net loss		(4,145)

Stocktaking and the valuation of stock is a very big subject and there is only room to mention the outline of a few key principles. Perhaps the most important is that, for reasons explained in Chapter 4, stock should be valued at the lower of cost and net realisable value. It is wrong to take a profit before a sale can legitimately be booked. Stock should be promptly written down if necessary to recognise obsolescence, damage, shrinkage etc. The described method of preparing the trading account means that stock lost or stolen is included in the cost of sales. If it is not there, it is not counted and the original cost is included in cost of sales.

Stock should be valued from period to period according to consistently applied principles. A change in the method of valuation will affect the profit. If there is a change, it should be for a good reason and the effect on the profit should be established. If the accounts are published, the effect of the change must be disclosed.

There are many ways of valuing stock but two competing principles should be mentioned:

First in first out (FIFO)

This assumes that the goods purchased first are sold first. This is a very commonly applied principle and has much to commend it. It does matter because over a period of time goods have probably been purchased at different prices.

Last in first out (LIFO)

This is the opposite to FIFO and assumes that the most recent purchases are sold first.

A manufacturing business

It was explained earlier in this chapter that the profit and loss account of a trading business must only contain the cost of the goods actually sold. The cost of goods purchased and held in stock must be excluded. For the same reason the profit and loss account of a manufacturing business must only contain the manufacturing costs of the goods actually sold in the period. The manufacturing costs of goods not sold must be excluded. As with a trading business it will probably be necessary to stocktake at the beginning and end of the period, but if controls are good and there have been efficient checks, it may not be necessary.

The profit and loss account of a manufacturing business has certain similarities with the profit and loss account of a trading business. The gross profit is the difference between sales and the manufacturing cost of the goods sold. The manufacturing cost includes the cost of raw materials, bought in components, and also such things as factory wages and the costs of the factory, such as power and depreciation of machinery.

Sometimes the manufacturing costs are shown in a separate manufacturing account. This leads to a manufacturing profit which is carried forward to the profit and loss account, with other costs being deducted in the profit and loss account. However, it is more common to have just the profit and loss account, with the manufacturing section set out at the top and leading to the manufacturing profit. This is best illustrated with a simplified example.

Bognor Cases Ltd manufactures and sells suitcases. Sales in the year to 30 June were £1,000,000. Purchases of materials and components in the year totalled £400,000. Stock at 30 June was £365,000 and at the previous 30 June it was £320,000.

Wages of production staff were £216,000. Factory rent was £110,000 and factory power costs were £40,000. Other production costs were £40,000. Salaries of salesmen, administration staff and management totalled £82,000. Other overheads were £66,000.

Bognor Cases Ltd
Profit and Loss Account for year to 30 June

	£	£
Sales		1,000,000
Opening stock	320,000	
Add purchases	400,000	
	720,000	
Less closing stock	365,000	
	355,000	
Production wages	216,000	
Factory rent	110,000	
Power costs	40,000	
Other production costs	40,000	
Cost of manufacturing		761,000
		239,000
Less overheads		
Salaries	82,000	
Other overheads	66,000	
		148,000
Net profit		91,000

Note that the costs are split into two sections. All costs relating to the product and manufacturing go into the top part. These contribute to the cost of manufacturing and to the subtotal which is the manufacturing profit. Overhead costs go below this subtotal.

The interpretation of accounts is covered in Chapter 10, but an obvious question is raised here. Despite what many would consider to be a good net profit, just why are stocks so high? They represent about a year's sales. An explanation from the managers would not be amiss.

Taxation and appropriation

'But in this world nothing can be said to be certain except death and taxes.'

Benjamin Franklin

You will probably recognise the words of the great and wise American statesman. He was a man of enormously varied interests, but although he was spot on with death and taxes, there were limits to his insight. In 1752, whilst studying electricity and lightning, he flew a kite in a thunderstorm to see if the electric charge would come down it.

The examples in this chapter have ended at the 'net profit' or 'net loss' stage, but better wording would be 'net profit before tax' or 'net loss before tax'. The tax charge must then be deducted to give 'net profit after tax'. If there has been a loss, it may be possible to add back a tax adjustment.

Appropriation is the dividing up of the profit after tax. In the case of a sole trader it is not necessary because it goes straight to the sole trader's capital account. It is important to ensure that appropriations are not classed as an expense, unlike interest which is an expense. It is a bad mistake to make.

The following is an example of the bottom part of the profit and loss account of a partnership. The partnership is Niven and Harvey. The two partners (Mr Niven and Mr Harvey) share profits equally.

	£
Profit before tax	130,000
Less tax	30,000
Profit after tax	100,000
Mr Niven 50%	50,000
Mr Harvey 50%	50,000

£50,000 is transferred to the accounts of each of the two partners. It might be more complicated because there may be interest on the partners' accounts, and there may be partners joining or leaving the partnership.

Questions to test your understanding

1. Bernard Smith starts work as a painter and decorator on 1 June. He does not hold stocks of materials as he buys just enough for each job. At the following 31 May his trial balance is as follows:

	Debit £	Credit £
Motor van	6,000	
Ladder and tools	1,000	
Bank account	300	
Trade debtors	700	
Trade creditors		400
Invoiced sales		15,000
Materials used	2,000	
Motor expenses	1,400	
Other overhead costs	4,000	
	15,400	15,400

Bernard Smith is advised that he should depreciate the motor van by 25%, and the ladder and tools by 10%.

He believes that half the trade debtors are an irrecoverable bad debt. He holds an invoice for materials for £600 and an overheads invoice for £200. Neither have been entered into the books. He has paid £500 for a year's insurance in advance.

A customer has complained about bad workmanship. Bernard Smith has agreed to spend £200 putting it right.

Prepare his profit and loss account for the year to 31 May.

2. North West Novelties Ltd manufactures and sells garden gnomes. Sales in the year to 30 April were £600,000. Purchases of materials totalled £200,000. Closing stock was £40,000 and opening stock was £50,000.

Production wages in the year were £280,000 and other production costs were £90,000. Total overheads were £60,000.

Prepare the profit and loss account for the year to 30 April.

INSTANT TIP

Only the cost of goods actually sold in the period should be entered into the profit and loss account. To do otherwise will distort the profit.

What exactly is a balance sheet?

A profit and loss account and balance sheet are the main (or sometimes even the only) constituent parts of a set of accounts, though they are often accompanied by reports and other information. The published accounts of a registered company, which are examined in Chapter 9, must be accompanied by more information. A profit and loss account establishes the profit or loss over a stated period of time. A balance sheet is a freeze-frame picture of the assets and liabilities as at a stated date, which is very often the last date of the profit and loss period. The topics covered are:

- What is a balance sheet?
- The concept of ownership.
- The layout of the balance sheet.
- The main balance sheet headings.
- The preparation of a profit and loss account and balance sheet.

What is a balance sheet?

You can help yourself remember the answer to this question by thinking of the literal meaning of the words 'balance' and 'sheet'.

Balance This means that the balance sheet must balance. There are two parts to it and each part must total to the same figure. Put another way, the sum of the debit balances must equal the sum of the credit balances. All the figures come from the extended trial balance. The balance sheet sounds like the trial balance but the income and expenditure accounts are not included. The balance sheet balances because one figure, being the difference between the income and expenditure accounts (which is of course the profit or loss) is transferred to the balance sheet.

Sheet Taken literally this means a sheet of paper on which the figures are listed.

In Chapter 2 it was shown that there are five different types of account, and in Chapter 7 it was shown that the income and expenditure accounts are extracted from the extended trial balance. These make up the profit and loss account. The balance sheet is a logical listing of the other three types of account, namely:

- Asset accounts   (normally debit balances)
- Liability accounts   (normally credit balances)
- Capital accounts   (normally credit balances)

The net profit or net loss at the bottom of the profit and loss account is added to the capital accounts. The result is that the balance sheet balances, which is essential.

The profit and loss account covers a stated period of time. If trading is continuing, the profit or loss would be different if the period were to be one day longer or shorter. The balance sheet is not like that and it does not cover a period of time. It is a listing of the balances on just one fixed date which is stated, usually the last day of the trading period.

The concept of ownership

Asset and liability accounts are relatively easy to understand, but the capital accounts may cause difficulties. Sometimes there may be just one account called the capital account. In other cases there may be several accounts. Examples in a company are:

- Share capital account.
- Share premium account.
- Revenue reserves.

The capital accounts represent the net worth of the business. This is the present book value of the owners' investment in the business, which is not the same thing as the value of their original investment. The owners are a different entity to the business itself. A registered company has a legal existence and personality separate from the shareholders who own it. This is not the case in a business owned by a sole trader, but in bookkeeping and accounting practice a sole trader's business is distinct from the sole trader personally. It follows that the net assets of a business owned by a sole trader are owing to the sole trader.

If a company is wound up, and if the assets and liabilities are worth book value and if the costs of winding up are ignored, the owners will be paid out exactly the value of the capital accounts. This is easy to understand in the case of a listed public company. If you own shares in Barclays Bank plc, you are not the same as the bank. You are just one of a very large number of its owners. The capital accounts in the books of Barclays Bank plc represent the money owing to you and the other shareholders. It is the value of the combined investment made by all the shareholders.

The principle is exactly the same in a one-man or one-woman business. Let us return to Sally Blanchflower, whose first profit and loss account was given in Chapter 7, and whose profit was £5,099. Sally Blanchflower the business is separate from Sally Blanchflower the person. She probably has two bank accounts, one for the business and one for her personal affairs. She may even pay herself a 'salary' from one bank account to the other, though technically a sole trader does not receive a salary. If her business is wound up, what is left after everything has been collected in and paid out belongs to her. The final cheque in the business bank account cheque book pays her the amount in the capital account.

This is the reason that the capital accounts are listed with the liabilities.

The layout of the balance sheet

Until the last 40 years or so it was the practice to set out the figures side by side. The assets (debit balances) were listed on the left and the liabilities (credit balances) were listed on the right. It is still occasionally done in this way but you will almost certainly see the balance sheets presented in a vertical format. The examples in this book are exclusively shown in this way.

A vertical balance sheet shows liabilities deducted from assets in a logical manner. The assets are stated in the order of their permanence, with fixed assets being shown before current assets and the same principle followed within fixed assets. For example, if a business owns freehold land and buildings, this will almost certainly be the most permanent asset. So it is usual to list this first within the category of fixed assets. The assets and liabilities add down to the 'net worth' of the business. The figure for net worth is represented by the capital accounts which are shown separately and have the same total.

This is best illustrated with an example. The following is the balance sheet of a partnership where the two partners share the profits equally:

Smith and Jones
Balance Sheet at 30 April

Fixed assets	£	£
Freehold property	200,000	
Plant and machinery	120,000	
Motor vehicles	40,000	
		360,000
Current assets		
Stock	170,000	
Trade debtors	130,000	
	300,000	
Less current liabilities		
Bank overdraft	60,000	
Trade creditors	120,000	
	180,000	
Net current assets		120,000
		480,000
Capital accounts		
Smith		240,000
Jones		240,000
		480,000

This is, of course, a simple balance sheet. In practice there would be several notes giving relevant details of how the figures are made up. Note that the net worth of the partnership is £480,000. If the partnership were to be wound up, if the assets and liabilities achieved book value and if there were no winding up expenses, Smith and Jones would get £240,000 each.

The main balance sheet headings

Of course not every individual account in the trial balance appears individually in the balance sheet. If it did, the balance sheet of a major company would be hundreds of pages long. The need for this is overcome by grouping accounts of a similar type. For example, the business may owe money to many suppliers, but just one figure for the total will appear in the balance sheet as 'trade creditors'.

An explanation of the main terms used in balance sheets follows. Where these terms appear in the Smith and Jones balance sheet shown in the previous section of this chapter, the corresponding figure is given.

Fixed assets

These assets are a capital investment. They will retain at least some of their value over the long term and will be available to generate revenue in the long term. The long term is usually taken to be a period longer than one year. It is not right to write them off to the profit and loss account immediately. Instead depreciation entries write them off over an appropriate period of time. Examples of fixed assets are freehold property, leasehold property, computers, fixtures and fittings, motor vehicles and plant and machinery.

The figure in the Smith and Jones balance sheet is £360,000. This will be the total amount paid for the freehold property, plant and machinery and the motor vehicles, less depreciation written off in the profit and loss account in the years since the assets were purchased.

In practice it is rare for fixed assets to be actually worth exactly their written-down value in the books. The reasons are:

- The arbitrary nature of the depreciation rules.
- Individual circumstances.
- Inflation.

Asset strippers specialise in finding companies where the fixed assets are worth more than the book value. They then purchase the company, and unlock the value by selling some or all of the assets and realising the profit.

Current assets

These are assets whose value is available to the business in the short term. This is either because they are part of the trading cycle (such as stock and trade debtors) or because they are short term investments (such as a 90-day bank deposit account). The definition of 'short term' is usually taken to be up to a year.

Debtors are usually current assets. The definition of a debtor is a person owing money to the business, such as a customer for goods sold. Examples of current assets are:

- Stock.
- Trade debtors.
- Bank accounts.
- Short-term investments.

The figure in the Smith and Jones balance sheet is £300,000.

Current liabilities

These are liabilities that the business could be called upon to discharge in the short term. The definition of 'short term' is usually taken to be up to a year. Examples are trade creditors, bank overdrafts, taxation payable within a year and hire purchase payable within a year. The definition of a creditor is a person to whom the business owes money, such as a supplier.

The figure in the Smith and Jones balance sheet is £180,000.

Net current assets

This is also known as working capital and it is extremely significant. It is the difference between current assets and current liabilities, and it can be a negative figure if the liabilities are greater.

It is very important, because net current assets are what is available to finance the day-to-day running of the business. If net current assets are insufficient for this purpose the business may have to close or seek some other form of finance. It is possible for a business to be profitable but have to close due to a shortage of working capital.

The figure in the Smith and Jones balance sheet is £120,000.

Long-term liabilities

The Smith and Jones example does not include one, but these are liabilities which are payable after more than a year. An example is a fixed-term bank loan. A business may be able to solve a shortage of working capital by obtaining a long-term loan in place of a bank overdraft.

Bank overdrafts are invariably legally repayable on demand. This means in theory, and very occasionally in practice, that the bank manager can demand repayment at 3 pm and if payment has not been received take action at 4 pm. On the other hand, a long-term fixed loan is only repayable when stipulated by the agreement and according to the conditions in the agreement.

Let us consider a ten-year loan of £1,000,000, repayable by ten equal annual instalments of £100,000. The balance sheet would show £900,000 under long-term liabilities and £100,000 under current liabilities. After a year, and one repayment, the balance sheet would show £800,000 under long-term liabilities and £100,000 under current liabilities. Hire purchase contract balances are split in the same way. The part repayable after a year is shown in long-term liabilities.

A business has an obvious incentive to make as many as possible of its liabilities, long-term liabilities. This eases the pressure on working capital.

Capital and reserves

This is the 'net worth' of the business and is the bottom part of the balance sheet. The total figure for capital and reserves is the balance sheet total. The top part of the balance sheet is 'net assets' and comes to the same total. The figure for Smith and Jones is £480,000.

Capital and reserves together represent the investment of the owners in the business. In the case of a company, capital and reserves may be made up of some combination of:

- Share capital: there may be more than one class of share.
- Revenue reserves: these are accumulated net profits from the past, after taxation, dividends and distributions.
- Capital reserves: these are reserves created in defined ways and only available for distribution in defined ways.
- Profit and loss account: this is part of revenue reserves.

The preparation of a profit and loss account and balance sheet

This section of the chapter shows how a profit and loss account and balance sheet of a company are produced from an extended trial balance. Shown below is the trial balance of Addic Services Ltd as at 30 September, the profit and loss account for the year to 30 September and the balance sheet as at 30 September. All the necessary adjustments have been made except for taxation, which will be 20% of the profit for the year. The accounts are not in a form suitable for publication. The trial balance is as follows.

Addic Services Ltd
Trial balance at 30 September

Debit balances	£	Credit balances	£
All overhead accounts	530,000	Fees invoiced – UK	600,000
Motor vehicles	62,000	Fees invoiced – Export	170,000
Freehold premises	389,000	Bank overdraft	68,000
Computer equipment	66,000	Trade creditors	101,000
Trade debtors	290,000	Taxation	13,000
Other debtors	24,000	Long-term loan	50,000
		Share capital	100,000
		Revenue reserves	259,000
	1,361,000		1,361,000

The necessary steps are:

1. The accounts of a profit and loss nature must be extracted from the trial balance and listed to form the profit and loss account as far as 'profit before tax'.
2. The taxation charge must be calculated and this should be deducted in the profit and loss account. This will give the figure for profit after tax and will complete the profit and loss account.
3. The taxation charge must be added to the Taxation account in the trial balance. This is money owing by the company and it is therefore a liability with a credit balance.
4. The profit after tax must be added to Revenue reserves.
5. The remaining accounts in the trial balance, which are all of a balance sheet nature, should be listed to form the balance sheet.

The resulting profit and loss account and balance sheet are as follows:

Addic Services Ltd
Profit and Loss Account for the Year to 30 September

	£
Fees invoiced – UK	600,000
Fees invoiced – Export	170,000
Total fees invoiced	770,000
Less all overheads	530,000
Profit before tax	240,000
Less taxation charge for the year	48,000
Net profit after tax	192,000

Addic Services Ltd
Balance Sheet as at 30 September

	£	£
Fixed assets		
Freehold premises	389,000	
Computer equipment	66,000	
Motor vehicles	62,000	
		517,000
Current assets		
Trade debtors	290,000	
Other debtors	24,000	
	314,000	
Less current liabilities		
Bank overdraft	68,000	
Trade creditors	101,000	
Taxation	61,000	
	230,000	
Net current assets		84,000
Long-term loan		(50,000)
		551,000
Capital employed		
Share capital		100,000
Revenue reserves	259,000	
Add profit for year after tax	192,000	
		451,000
		551,000

The long-term loan is a liability and has a credit balance in the trial balance. This is why the figure is in brackets and deducted from the assets.

The revenue reserves figure of £259,000 is at the previous balance sheet date. The figure of £451,000 will be the opening balance for revenue reserves in the next period.

Shareholders' funds are £551,000, which is the same as the 'net worth' of the company at book value. If there are 100,000 shares in issue, each one is backed by net assets of £5.51.

Questions to test your understanding

1. Does a balance sheet record what has happened over a period of time?
2. As at the balance sheet date payments of £60,000 are outstanding on a hire purchase contract. The £60,000 is payable in 24 equal monthly instalments over 2 years. How much of the £60,000 should be included in current liabilities?
3. The trial balance of Peter Harvey, who is a sole trader, is as shown opposite at 31 March.

   All the adjustments have been made. Prepare the profit and loss account for the year to 31 March and the balance sheet at that date. Ignore taxation.

	Debit £	Credit £
Bad debts written off	240	
Bank account	22,198	
Capital account		10,632
Charitable donations	200	
Depreciation	2,500	
Depreciation on motor vehicle		5,000
Electricity	270	
Insurance	590	
Motor vehicle	10,000	
Office expenses	1,660	
Postage	168	
Rent	2,000	
Sales		28,776
Telephone	413	
Travel expenses	3,988	
Trade creditors		661
Trade debtors	842	
	45,069	45,069

INSTANT TIP

The profit and loss account measures activity over a period. The balance sheet presents the assets and the liabilities at a certain date.

What should I know about published reports and accounts?

Important point: This chapter relates to accounts published in Britain. The laws are different in other countries.

The aim of this chapter is to summarise the information disclosed in a published set of reports and accounts, and to give hints on what to look for and the significance of what you will see. It will probably be considered the most detailed chapter in the book, and it should therefore be looked upon as something of a challenge.

To get the best out of this chapter it is a good idea to have a set of reports and accounts to hand. You will then be able to check the various points in them. It is an even better idea to have the reports and accounts for a company that you know well, and your employer is an obvious example of such a company. The accounts of any registered company can be obtained from Companies House and the first section of this chapter explains how this can be done.

Two cautions may be necessary. Firstly, published accounts are by definition out of date. Secondly, do not neglect the notes. The topics studied in this chapter are:

- The obligation to publish accounts.
- Accounting standards.
- Profit and loss account and notes.
- Balance sheet and notes.
- Cash flow statement.
- Directors' report.
- Directors' remuneration report.
- The audit report.
- Group accounts.

The obligation to publish accounts

The directors of all companies, including even dormant companies, are required by law to prepare statutory reports and accounts, and in all cases they are required to send them to the members. In the great majority of companies the terms 'member' and 'shareholder' are virtually interchangeable. In the case of public companies the directors must lay the accounts at a shareholders' meeting, usually the annual general meeting. It is no longer necessary to lay the accounts in private companies, but it must be done if it is required by the articles.

Having a company is a privilege and having a limited liability company is a very considerable privilege. In return for this privilege it is a requirement that the reports and accounts be made available to the suppliers, bank, creditors and the public in general. Directors do this by sending them to Companies House where, for a modest charge, anyone can see them and obtain copies. Companies incorporated in England and Wales file at Companies House in Cardiff. Companies incorporated in Scotland file at Companies House in Edinburgh. The contact details are:

England and Wales:
Companies House
Crown Way
Maindy
Cardiff
CF14 3UZ
Tel: 0870 333 3636
Website:
www.companieshouse.gov.uk

Scotland:
Companies House
37 Castle Terrace
Edinburgh
EH21 2ED
Tel: 0870 333 3636
Website:
www.companieshouse.gov.uk

Copies may be obtained by using the website, telephone, post or by personal visit. There is also a Companies House office at 21 Bloomsbury Street, London WC1B 3XD. The telephone and website details are the same as for the other two offices.

Quoted companies must, for accounting periods starting on or after 6 April 2008, place their accounts on a website which is freely available to the public.

Small and medium-sized companies may file abbreviated accounts at Companies House, though full accounts must be sent to the members. However, the full accounts may omit certain information that it is compulsory to disclose in the accounts of larger companies.

A small company (subject to certain exceptions) is one that in two successive years (counted on a group basis) satisfies any two of turnover not more than £5.6 million, balance sheet total not more than £2.8 million and 50 employees. For accounting periods commencing on or after 6 April 2008 the turnover figure is £6.5 million and the balance sheet figure is £3.26 million.

A medium-sized company (subject to certain exceptions) is one that in two successive years (counted on a group basis) satisfies any two of turnover £22.8 million, balance sheet total £11.4 million and 250 employees. For accounting periods commencing on or after 6 April 2008 the turnover figure is £25.9 million and the balance sheet total is £12.9 million.

Small and medium-sized companies need not send a profit and loss account or directors' report to Companies House and the balance sheet may be abbreviated. Medium-sized companies must send more to Companies House but they need not disclose turnover, other operating income or cost of sales. However, for accounts periods commencing on or after 6 April 2008 they must disclose turnover. Both small and medium-sized companies must send full accounts to their members.

Every company has an accounting reference date and the directors must prepare accounts with reference to it, including a balance sheet dated within seven days either side of it. Counting from the accounting reference date, a quoted public company has six months to deliver the accounts to Companies House and lay them in a meeting. An unlisted public company has seven months to do the same. A private company has ten months to deliver them to Companies House and to the members. For accounts periods commencing on or after 6 April 2008 these periods are reduced to six months, six months and nine months respectively.

The accounts of all companies must be formally approved by the board and the balance sheet must be signed by any director. The directors' report too must be formally approved by the board and it must be signed by any director or the company secretary.

Accounting standards

The first accounting standards were issued in the late 1960s and they have been extensively developed ever since. They are intended to ensure that accounts are prepared according to sensible and consistently applied rules, and that the accounts of different companies are prepared in a comparable way and can therefore be properly and usefully compared. The list of standards is now long and comprehensive.

UK standards are issued by the Accounting Standards Board and are known as Financial Reporting Standards (abbreviated to FRS). International Accounting Standards are issued by the International Accounting Standards Board. Quoted companies are required to use international standards and AIM listed companies have been required to do so for financial periods commencing on or after 1 January 2007. Other companies may use UK standards but there is a trend towards the use of international standards. A very studious person has calculated that the introduction of international accounting standards has, on average, resulted in an increase of nearly 60% in the length of the reports and accounts package, and the average length has subsequently increased still further.

Directors have an overall responsibility to ensure that the accounts give a 'true and fair view' and this overrides all other considerations. It is not a specific legal requirement that accounts conform with applicable accounting standards. However, accounts almost always do conform with applicable accounting standards. This is partly because accounting standards are generally respected, partly because failure to comply would generate suspicious questions and partly because it would result in a qualified audit report. Very occasionally directors do deviate from accounting standards and give their reasons for doing so. There must be a statement in the notes to the accounts as to whether the accounts have been prepared in accordance with applicable accounting standards. Furthermore, the notes must give particulars of any material departure from the standards and the reasons for the departure must be given.

Accounting standards can make a big difference. There was a furore some years ago when FRS17 took effect. This standard applied to retirement benefits and forced companies in some circumstances to recognise pension fund deficits in their accounts. This had a dramatic impact on the reported figures of some companies, British Airways plc being just one significant example. It was very controversial and is perhaps one of the reasons that many companies have been trying to withdraw from defined benefit pension schemes. Of course FRS17 did not affect the underlying reality – only the way that the deficits were recognised and the figures reported. Despite its detractors this seems an excellent reason for its adoption. This standard, and its international equivalent, have received the most public attention, but other standards too have been very significant.

The international standard IAS19 is the equivalent of FRS17. It has many similarities but is less rigid in forcing companies to immediately recognise deficits in their balance sheets.

A list of international accounting standards, correct at the time of writing, is given in Appendix A of this book. An up-to-date list may be obtained from **www.iasb.org**. On the left side, click the link to IFRS summaries and then, if wished, to IFRS and IAS summaries in English.

A list of UK accounting standards, correct at the time of writing, is given in Appendix B of this book. An up-to-date list may be obtained from **www.frrp.org.uk/asb** then follow the links to accounting standards board.

Profit and loss account and notes

The profit and loss account must be laid out in the way required by law and accounting standards, and it must be accompanied by notes that give certain information required by law and accounting standards. Figures for both the current period and previous period must be given. Following is the key part of a recent profit and loss account (entitled 'Consolidated Income Statement') of a major British company. It has been prepared in accordance with international financial reporting standards.

Your first reaction may well be that, although the key figures are given, for a company with an annual turnover in excess of seven billion pounds there is not much detail. When I tell you that the company's complete reports and accounts package occupies 105 A4-sized pages this feeling may be even stronger. You may also wonder if 105 pages is really necessary and you will not be the only person to have had this thought. To a considerable extent we must blame (or thank) accounting standards, especially international financial reporting standards. We live in inflationary times regarding the publication of words and figures. It is interesting to note that the Bible reports the ten commandments in 319 words, whereas the Companies Act 2006 takes 305,397 words. Even non-Christians would probably concede that the ten commandments have had the greater impact on the human race.

Consolidated Income Statement

	Notes	Current Year	Previous Year
Revenue	2	7,797.7	7,490.5
Operating profit			
Before exceptional operating charges		850.1	648.7
Exceptional operating charges		–	(50.6)
	2, 3	850.1	598.1
Interest payable and similar charges	5	(134.9)	(120.9)
Interest receivable	5	30.5	27.9
Profit on ordinary activities before taxation		745.7	505.1
Analysed between:			
Before exceptional operating charges and property disposals		751.4	556.1
Loss on property disposals	3	(5.7)	(0.4)
Exceptional operating charges	3	–	(50.6)
Income tax expense	6	(225.1)	(150.1)
Profit on ordinary activities after taxation		520.6	355.0
Profit from discontinued operations	7A	2.5	231.2
Profit for the year attributable to shareholders		523.1	586.2

Of course much more information is given in the notes. This includes a geographical and segmental split of the revenue. A further note splits the profit before interest figure of £850.1 million as follows:

	£m
Revenue	7,797.7
Cost of sales	(4,812.1)
Gross profit	2,985.6
Selling and marketing expenses	(1,625.7)
Administrative expenses	(522.7)
Other operating income	18.6
Loss on property disposals	(5.7)
Operating profit after exceptional items	850.1

It goes on to give the following further split:

	Selling and marketing expenses £m	Admini- strative expenses £m	Total £m
Employee costs (see note 10A)	844.9	228.3	1,073.2
Occupancy costs	276.2	49.2	325.4
Repairs, renewals and maintenance of property	73.0	17.2	90.2
Depreciation and amortisation	243.5	30.5	274.0
Other costs	188.1	197.5	385.6
Operating expenses before exceptional items	1,625.7	522.7	2,148.4

It is not reproduced above but the same note gives the corresponding analysis for the previous year.

You will see that the profit and loss information disclosed in the notes is building up and there is much more. Compulsory disclosure (where applicable) must include the following:

Extraordinary income and expenditure

These are separate from the ordinary activities of the company and must be separated from the ordinary activities. They are not usually encountered. A very hypothetical example could be the income and expenditure of a chain of florists' shops opened and closed by a quarrying company.

Exceptional income and expenditure

These are derived from ordinary activities, but are exceptional because of their size or some other factor. The redundancy and other costs of closing a division of the company could be an example of this.

Prior year adjustments

These could be necessitated by the discovery of a fundamental error in previous accounts or by a change in accounting policy. The policy on valuing stocks is a possible example of the latter as this affects reported profits. Classifying an asset account as an income account could be an example of a fundamental error. The risks of this and similar mistakes were examined in Chapter 1.

Interest payable and receivable and similar

Interest payable must be analysed between the following categories:

- Amounts payable on bank loans and overdrafts.
- Loans of any other kind made to the company.
- Lease finance charges allocated for the year.

Gains and losses on the repurchase or early settlement of debt should be separately disclosed as should the unwinding of any discount on provisions.

Income from listed investments

Rent receivable in connection with land

Payments for the hire of plant and machinery

Details of auditors' remuneration

This must be split as follows:

- Remuneration (inclusive of sums paid in respect of expenses).
- The aggregate of other fees paid to the auditors and their associates, with a split showing the categories of services provided.
- The nature of any benefit in kind provided to the auditors.

The amount paid to auditors for consultancy and other services can sometimes be a matter of controversy. It may be bigger than the audit fee which, big as the figure may seem, might even be considered a loss leader. Some people wonder if in these circumstances auditors can really be objective. Auditors of course insist that they can, not least because they have so much to lose if they are not.

Employees

The average number of persons employed by the company in the year, determined on a monthly basis, must be shown. There must be an analysis between appropriate categories, as determined by the directors, of the monthly number of employees.

The aggregate amounts for the period must be shown of wages and salaries, social security costs and other pension costs.

The basis of any foreign currency translation

Details of any transfers to and from reserves

Appropriations (including dividends)

Details must be given of:

- The aggregate amount of dividends paid and proposed.
- The amount set aside or proposed to be set aside to, or withdrawn or proposed to be withdrawn, from reserves.
- The amounts set aside for redemption of share capital or for redemption of loans.
- The aggregate of dividends for each class of share.
- The amount of any appropriation of profits in respect of non-equity shares other than dividends.

Government grants

The effect of Government grants on the results for the period must be shown.

Capitalisation, depreciation, amortisation and impairment

Directors' remuneration

There are separate requirements for quoted companies but the following must be given for other companies:

- Amounts paid to or receivable by directors in respect of qualifying services.
- Amounts paid to or receivable by directors in respect of long-term incentive schemes.
- Any company contributions paid to pension schemes.

The following must be disclosed if the aggregate directors' emoluments are £200,000 or higher:

- The emoluments of the highest paid director.
- The value of the company contributions paid, or treated as paid, to a money purchase pension scheme in respect of the highest paid director.
- Where the highest paid director is a member of a defined benefit pension scheme, and has performed pensionable qualifying services in the year:
  - the amount at the end of the year of the accrued pension; and
  - the amount at the end of the year of the accrued lump sum.
- If the highest paid director exercised any share options in the year, then a statement of this fact.
- If the highest paid director received, or became entitled to receive, any shares under a long-term incentive scheme, then a statement of that fact.

Definitions are important and there is more detail, but the above is a working summary. For obvious reasons this section of the notes is often studied with particular interest.

Pension costs

Taxation

An analysis of tax payable must be given. There are lengthy detailed requirements.

Balance sheet and notes

Like the profit and loss account the balance sheet must be laid out in the way required by law and accounting standards, and it must be accompanied by notes that give certain information required by law and accounting standards. Comparative figures as at the start of the profit and loss period must be given. Following is the balance sheet of the major British company whose profit and loss account was featured in the previous section.

Consolidated Balance Sheet

	Notes	Current year £m	Previous year £m
ASSETS			
Non-current assets			
Intangible assets	13	163.5	165.4
Property, plant and equipment	14	3,575.8	3,586.2
Investment property	15	38.5	38.6
Investments in joint venture	16	9.0	8.7
Other financial assets	17	3.3	0.3
Trade and other receivables	18	242.8	211.2
Deferred income tax assets	25	35.5	24.6
		4,068.4	4,035.0
Current assets			
Inventories		374.3	338.9
Other financial assets	17	48.8	67.0
Trade and other receivables	18	210.5	213.8
Derivative financial instruments	22	76.4	–
Cash and cash equivalents	19	362.6	212.6
Assets of discontinued operation	7C	69.5	–
		1,142.1	832.3
Total assets		5,210.5	4,867.3

LIABILITIES
Current liabilities

Trade and other payables	20	867.8	717.9
Derivative financial instruments	22	8.0	–
Borrowings	21	1,052.8	478.8
Current tax liabilities		58.7	15.5
Provisions	24	9.2	25.2
Liabilities of discontinued operation	7C	20.5	–
		2,017.0	1,237.4

Non-current liabilities

Borrowings	21	1,133.8	1,948.5
Retirement benefit obligations	11	794.9	676.0
Other non-current liabilities	20	74.8	71.8
Derivative financial instruments	22	9.5	–
Provisions	24	19.1	19.7
Deferred income tax liabilities	25	6.1	4.7
		2,038.2	2,720.7
Total liabilities		4,055.2	3,958.1
Net assets		1,155.3	909.2

EQUITY

Called-up share capital – equity	26, 27	420.6	414.5
Called-up share capital – non-equity	27	–	65.7
Share premium account	27	162.3	106.6
Capital redemption reserve	27	2,113.8	2,102.8
Hedging reserve	27	(8.0)	–
Other reserves	27	(6,542.2)	(6,542.2)
Retained earnings	27	5,008.8	4,761.8
Total equity		1,155.3	909.2

You will no doubt notice that every line is cross-referenced to a note. Notes must (where applicable) include the following:

Details of share capital and debentures

This includes separate details of authorised and issued capital, details of any debentures and information about redeemable preference shares.

Details of tangible fixed assets and depreciation

Details of investments

Separate details for quoted and unquoted investments must be given. Details of aggregate market value must be given if this differs from the balance sheet value.

Details of movements in reserves and provisions

Details of indebtedness

Convertible debt should be analysed between amounts falling due:

- In one year or less, or on demand.
- Between one and two years.
- Between two and five years.
- In five years or more.

In respect of debt that is due for repayment wholly or partly after five years, terms of interest and repayment should be stated. So too should details of any security given. There are further requirements.

Details of any cumulative dividends in arrears

Details of any guarantees given

Details of capital commitments and other commitments at the balance sheet date

Details of contingent liabilities at the balance sheet date

Debtors

The analysis must separate sums falling due within one year from sums falling due after one year.

Post-balance sheet events

For non-adjusting post-balance sheet events and the reversal of a transaction which was entered into to alter the appearance of the balance sheet it is necessary to show:

- The nature of the event.
- An estimate of the financial effect, or a statement that it is not practicable to make such an estimate.
- An explanation of the taxation implications, where necessary for a proper understanding of the financial position.

Cash flow statement

Cash is not the same as profit, a point that is sometimes overlooked. The distinction is very important. For all but small companies a cash flow statement is required as part of the reports and accounts package.

The purpose of the cash flow statement is to spotlight the increase or decrease in cash between two balance sheet dates. It gives the total for the movement and shows how an adverse movement has been financed or a positive movement applied. It also shows in detail the various factors that have contributed to the movement. An example of just one of the calculations is the following:

Trade debtors at latest balance sheet	£830,000
Trade debtors at previous balance sheet	£880,000
Cash inflow	£50,000

A cash inflow has arisen because the company is owed less money at the date of the latest balance sheet. This could have been caused by a number of factors and it is not necessarily a reason for satisfaction. Perhaps the company has been more efficient at collecting its debts or perhaps it has started offering discounts for prompt payment. Perhaps trade is down and there are less debts to collect. Perhaps the workforce has been on strike and there have been no deliveries to customers in the month leading up to the second balance sheet date. Perhaps last year's figure was bad rather than this year's figure good.

Capital expenditure and dividends are examples of payments that take cash out of the company without having an effect, apart from depreciation in the case of capital expenditure, on profit.

Professional analysts always pay a great deal of attention to the cash flow statement, especially if they believe that the company may be short of working capital. Readers of relatively advanced years and with long memories may remember the turmoil in Britain in the 1970s. At that time there was a widespread catchphrase, sometimes attributed to Jim Slater of Slater Walker fame, that *'Cash is King'*. It was certainly true that companies that controlled their cash did not fold in the way that so many others did. Another memorable phrase popular in the 1970s and subsequently is *'profit is a matter of opinion whereas cash is a matter of fact'*. Anyone who studied the Enron accounts would have done well to have kept it in mind.

The summary cash flow statement for the company whose profit and loss account and balance sheet was reproduced earlier is as follows:

Operating activities

Operating profit before exceptional operating charges	850.1
Depreciation and amortisation	274.0
Share-based payments	24.7
Loss on property disposals	5.7
(Increase)/decrease in inventories	(42.2)
Increase in receivables	(4.1)
Payments to acquire leasehold properties	(38.0)
Increase/(decrease) in payables	128.0
Exceptional operating cash outflow	(14.6)
Cash inflow from continuing operations	1,183.6
Cash inflow from discontinued operations	13.9
Cash inflow from operating activities	1,197.5
Net interest paid	(129.9)
Tax paid	(101.5)
Capital expenditure and financial investment	(267.3)
Acquisitions and disposals	–
Equity dividends paid	(204.1)
Purchase of own shares	–
Other transactions with shareholders	55.8
Debt financing net of liquid resources disposed with subsidiary	–
Exchange and other movements	(2.6)
Change in net debt	547.9
Opening net debt	(2,147.7)
Reclassification under IFRS	(129.5)
Closing net debt	(1,729.3)

Directors' report

It is a legal requirement that certain information must be disclosed in the directors' report. The list includes the following but the first four items are not required if it is a small company:

1. *An indication (if applicable) of the existence of branches within the European Union.*
2. *Details of any important events since the year end.*
3. *The amount of recommended dividends.*
4. *Any difference in market value of interests in land or buildings over book value at the balance sheet date.* This is only if the directors believe that the members' attention should be drawn to it and in practice it is usually only done if the difference is material.
5. *The names of all persons who were directors during the year.* If a person was not a director for the whole of the year, the date of appointment and/or the date of resignation or removal must be given.
6. *Political donations.* If expenditure on political purposes in the year exceeds £200, details of amounts and the name of each person or organisation receiving such amounts must be given. A wholly owned subsidiary company need not give this information, but it must be given by the holding company. The disclosure threshold is increased to £2,000 for accounts periods commencing on or after 6 April 2008.
7. *Charitable donations.* If expenditure on charitable purposes in the year exceeds £200, details must be given. Expenditure on charitable purposes outside of Great Britain is excluded for this purpose. A wholly owned subsidiary company need not give this information, but it must be given by the holding company. The disclosure threshold is increased to £2,000 for accounts periods commencing on or after 6 April 2008.

8. *Changes in share capital.* This is the issue of new shares and the acquisition of its own shares.
9. *Payment of suppliers.* The following must be given for public companies and for large private companies that are subsidiaries of public companies:
   (a) A statement of policy on the payment of suppliers.
   (b) If the company subscribes to a code on payment practices, such as the CBI code, this must be stated, and it must also be stated how details of the code may be obtained.
   (c) A statement of the average number of days' credit outstanding at the balance sheet date.
   It is not unknown for companies to 'window dress' the ratio by making extensive payments just before the balance sheet date.
10. *Accounting principles.* Details of accounting principles adopted must be given.
11. *Going concern.* If applicable, directors should report:
    (a) Any material uncertainties, of which the directors are aware, in making their assessment of the going concern status of the company, that may cast significant doubt on the company's ability to continue as a going concern.
    (b) Where the foreseeable future considered by the directors in their assessment of the going concern status of the company is less than one year from the date of approval of the financial statements, then that fact.
    (c) Where the financial statements are not prepared on a going concern basis, that fact, together with the basis on which the financial statements are prepared and the reasons why the company is not considered a going concern.
12. *Statement as to disclosure to auditors.* Section 418(2) of the Companies Act 2006 states:
    'The directors' report must contain a statement to the

effect that, in the case of each of the persons who are directors at the time the report is approved –

(a) so far as the director is aware, there is no relevant audit information of which the company's auditor is unaware, and

(b) he has taken all the steps that he ought to have taken as a director in order to make himself aware of any relevant audit information and to establish that the company's auditor is aware of that information.'

This, of course, only applies if the accounts are audited.

13. *Business review.* This is required for all but small companies and it must contain:

(a) A fair review of the company's business.

(b) A description of the principal risks and uncertainties facing the company.

(c) The development and performance of the company's business during the financial year.

(d) The position of the company's business at the end of the year, consistent with the size and complexity of the business.

Considerably more information is required if the company is a quoted company and if the period commenced on or after 1 October 2007. This includes:

(a) The main trends and factors likely to affect the future development, performance and position of the company's business.

(b) Information about environmental matters, the company's employees and social and community issues.

(c) Information about persons with whom the company has contractual or other arrangements which are essential to the business of the company. However, this is not required if disclosure would, in the opinion of the directors, be seriously prejudicial to that person and contrary to the public interest.

Directors' remuneration report

This is required for quoted companies only and, human nature being what it is, it often seems to be the most studied part of the reports and accounts package. The report must contain a mass of information about the salary, bonus, pension, share options, service contract, etc. of each director by name.

There must be a separate vote on the directors' remuneration report at the meeting at which the accounts are laid. However, the vote is advisory and does not change anything, though a vote to reject the report may be massively damaging and have a major persuasive effect. This actually happened in GlaxoSmithKline plc a few years ago and it almost happened in British Airways plc.

The audit report

Every company is required to have an auditor, subject to limited exceptions for small companies and dormant companies. The primary function of an auditor is to report on the statutory accounts. It should particularly be noted that they report on the accounts and express an opinion. They do not certify the accuracy of the figures. This is very widely misunderstood by the public and by some managers too.

The prime purpose of an audit report is to state whether, in the opinion of the auditor, the financial statements give a 'true and fair view'. Audit reports almost always do say this – the main reason being the skill, integrity and professionalism of directors. However, a seriously qualified audit report can be very damaging and directors therefore have a strong incentive to make any necessary changes. Some qualifications to an audit report may not be serious, such as, perhaps, a minor and technical breach of an accounting standard. The combined code calls for listed companies to set up an audit committee and many other companies choose to do this.

Group accounts

When two or more companies form a group, the parent company is required to issue group accounts as well as accounts just for itself. These must include a group profit and loss account and a group balance sheet, and they eliminate intra trading and intergroup indebtedness. The balance sheet shows the group's position vis-à-vis the outside world.

To understand why this is necessary consider three companies – **A**, **B** and **C**, with **B** and **C** being owned by **A**. **A** sells goods costing £600 to **B** for £1,000 but they have not yet been sold by **B**. Furthermore **A** has lent £1,000 to **B**, **B** has lent £1,000 to **C** and **C** has lent £1,000 to **A**. Without group accounts, **A** would declare £400 profit by effectively trading with itself and each company's balance sheet would have an extra £1,000 in both assets and liabilities.

Questions to test your understanding

1. Is it possible to obtain a copy of the accounts of a small company?
2. What is the consideration that overrides all other considerations, including accounting standards?
3. May a published profit and loss account be laid out in a way that discloses all the required information, but with profit after tax at the top?
4. May a balance sheet group debts due for immediate payment with debts due for payment in four years' time?
5. Mrs A served as a director for just four days in the middle of the accounting period. Must this be disclosed in the directors' report?

6. Must the business review (part of the directors' report) report on the main trends and factors likely to affect the future development, performance and position of the company's business?

7. How long does a private company have to deliver its accounts to Companies House, assuming that they relate to a financial period commencing on or after 6 April 2008?

INSTANT TIP

Do not forget that published accounts are a historical record. They are, by definition, out of date.

In what practical ways can I use published accounts?

In the case of registered companies the publication of accounts is a legal obligation and so is the publication of other information in a directors' report and, in some cases, elsewhere. Publication is also a legal obligation for some other organisations. Although most of the content of this chapter is of general application, it concentrates on the accounts of registered companies.

A main purpose of accounts is to provide a historical record, which is, of course, out of date when it is studied. This historical record is important and so is the opportunity to analyse the figures – to get behind them, understand them and use them in practical ways. Accounting ratios are a key tool in doing this, and a study of accounting ratios is the main point of this chapter. The subjects and ratios covered are:

Preparation

- How to obtain published accounts.
- How to get the best results.
- Proceed with care.

Profit ratios

- Profit to turnover.
- Gross profit margin.
- Interest cover.

Balance sheet ratios

- Gearing.
- Liquidity.
- Stock turn.

Investment ratios

- Return on capital employed.
- Dividend cover.
- Dividend yield.
- Earnings per share.
- Price earnings ratio.

Other ratios

- Number of days' credit given.
- Number of days' credit taken.

Following are a profit statement and balance sheet for Cotswold Components plc, together with some other information. The accounts are not in a form suitable for publication. The accounting ratios studied in this chapter are illustrated with reference to these accounts.

Cotswold Components plc
Profit Statement for the year to 31 December

	£000
Turnover	36,129
Cost of sales	22,116
Gross profit	14,013
Net operating expenses	9,664
Operating profit	4,349
Interest payable	412
Profit before tax	3,937
Tax	922
Profit after tax	3,015
Dividends	920
Retained profit for year	2,095

Cotswold Components plc
Balance Sheet at 31 December

	£000	£000
Fixed assets		3,777
Current assets		
Stock	2,116	
Trade debtors	6,724	
Investments	66	
	8,906	
Current liabilities		
Trade creditors	2,415	
Bank	4,300	
	6,715	
Net current assets		2,191
		5,968
Capital and reserves		
Called-up share capital		1,000
Profit and loss account		4,968
		5,968

Other information

1. The company has issued 10,000,000 ordinary shares of 10 pence each.
2. The current share price is £1.64.

How to obtain published accounts

There are approximately 2,500,000 companies in Britain registered at Companies House and, apart from fewer than 5,000 unlimited companies, the accounts of all of them are available to the public. You are the public, or at least part of it, and you can easily obtain a copy of the accounts of a company that interests you. You will need either the company's exact registered name or its registered number. There are two main methods:

- *From the Companies House website*: **www.companieshouse.gov.uk**. The cost is £1.00 to download a document.
- *By telephone*: 0870 333 3636. There is a charge of £3.00 which may be paid by credit card. Delivery is normally the following day.

How to get the best results

By definition an accounting ratio is the comparison of two figures, with the result expressed as a ratio or a percentage. In many cases there is general acceptance of the two figures to be compared and these ratios are explained in this chapter. However, there is nothing to stop you varying the definition of the figures to be compared. The use of 'profit before tax' rather than 'profit after tax' is an obvious example. Furthermore, there is nothing to stop you inventing your own comparisons and ratios.

Accounting ratios are very much a hands-on, practical matter. A certain amount of work is necessary and attention to detail is important. Mistakes are possible and there may be traps, some of which are explained in the next section of this chapter. Sometimes the analysis and conclusions are so obvious that they almost jump out of the page at you, but at other times they have to be unearthed with diligent and skilful work. You should try to be methodical and just a little sceptical, and you should keep the following points in mind.

Ask the question 'so what?'

When you have calculated a ratio it may tell you everything that you wanted to know and, if so, you can stop right there. For example, perhaps you had decided to sell some shares if the dividend yield was less than a certain percentage. However, a ratio is usually more useful if it is compared with another equivalent calculation. It might be helpful to compare it with such things as:

- Last year's results.
- The budget.
- The industry or sector average.
- The accounts of a competitor.

Be suspicious

Financial statements are prepared according to rules and assumptions. If different rules and assumptions are used, different results will be obtained. Published financial statements may legitimately, within certain limits, use different rules and assumptions, which in most cases must be stated. There are only self-imposed restraints relating to data prepared for internal management purposes.

In some cases the correct profit is a matter of opinion and this can also be true of many of the assets and liabilities. Cash, however, is almost entirely a matter of fact. It is there or it is not there. You should always approach your examination in a sceptical and enquiring state of mind.

Look for reasons

There may be special reasons that should be taken into account when the significance of a ratio is assessed. For example, very high expenditure on advertising right at the end of the financial period may reduce profits for the period, but hold out the promise of higher sales and profits in the next period. Of course it may do no such thing. The founder of Unilever famously remarked that he knew that half of his company's massive expenditure on advertising was wasted, but he did not know which half.

Look for trends

Trends may be more significant than a single comparison made at a fixed date. Fortunately, published accounts of companies are required by law to give corresponding figures for the previous period, so it is possible to plot a trend over at least a year. The published accounts of quoted companies will give certain key information over a period of five years.

A deteriorating payment performance, for example, often indicates liquidity problems, although it can also mean that selfish managers are hoarding cash at the expense of suppliers. If a company has gone from paying in 30 days to paying in 90 days, it may be more worrying than if it has consistently taken 90 days to pay.

Be open-minded

Do not have too many preconceived ideas. Be receptive to the unexpected.

Look at the notes and the accounting policies

You may be familiar with the saying *'the large print giveth and the small print taketh away'*. Professional analysts always spend time studying the notes to published accounts and the accounting policies. You should do the same and you should pay particular attention to any changes in accounting policies. Laws and accounting standards govern certain information that must be disclosed in the notes to published accounts of companies, and also in the directors' report.

Proceed with care

In the last section of this chapter you were advised to *'look for reasons'*. This section expands on that advice and details some of the traps that may be encountered.

Applying percentages to small base figures

David Lloyd George, a former British Prime Minister, once asked a civil servant to produce some statistics. The reply was 'certainly – what would you like me to prove?' Statistics and ratios can be misleading, especially when small base figures are used. This is best illustrated with an example. Suppose that a company has a turnover of £1 million in two successive years. The profit in the first year is £100 and the profit in the second year is £200. It would be true to say that the profit had doubled, but such a claim should be viewed in the context of the very low profit figures involved.

Failure to take full account of the notes and other information

It is sometimes said that professional analysts spend more time studying the notes to the accounts than they spend studying the actual accounts. This could be wise of them because the accounts are often just the starting point. As already mentioned above, in Britain (as in nearly all other countries) the law and various accounting standards specify a great deal of information that must be disclosed in the notes to the published accounts.

Failure to take account of a change in accounting policy

A change in accounting policy may affect the figures and the ratios, without there being any change in the underlying reality. Examples include changes in depreciation policy and changes in the way that stock is valued. The profit is the same in the long term, but the declared profit will be different in the year that the change is made. Fortunately, notes to the published accounts of companies must disclose significant changes in accounting policies and spell out the consequences.

Consider a company that two years ago purchased a piece of machinery for £500,000 and in the first year depreciated it by 25%. In the second year the company changed its policy and depreciated it by 20%. Clearly, the declared net profit before tax will be £25,000 higher than if the change had not been made.

Not always comparing like with like

The most recent (at the time of writing) accounts of Marks and Spencer Group plc disclose the following:

Sales for year (in £ million)	8,588.1
Trade receivables	67.9

You can easily work out that customers take an average of 2.9 days to pay for their purchases. The calculation is:

$$\frac{67.9 \times 365}{8,588.1} = 2.9 \text{ days}$$

You may think that this is stunningly good, and that the company must employ the world's best credit controllers. This may or may not be true, but it should not be deduced from these figures. The reason for this is that the company is in the retail sector and the great majority of sales are made for cash. Trade receivables should really be compared with just the part of sales that are made on credit.

Now consider the widget manufacturer whose accounts disclose the following:

Sales for year	£900,000
Trade debtors at the balance sheet date	£100,000

This appears to show that customers take an average of 40.6 days to pay. The calculation is:

$$\frac{100,000 \times 365}{900,000} = 40.6$$

This too is probably wrong because sales will almost certainly exclude VAT, and trade debtors will probably include it. If trade debtors all include 17.5% VAT, the correct calculation is:

$$\frac{85,106 \times 365 \text{ days}}{900,000} = 34.5 \text{ days}$$

85,106 is 100,000 with the 17.5% VAT removed.

Forgetting that some things can only be known by insiders

Published financial statements reveal a great deal, but there are some things that can only be known by those with inside information. Consider two companies that manufacture and sell screws:

	Company A	Company B
Sales	£3,900,000	£3,700,000
Cost of sales	£2,184,000	£2,146,000
Gross margin	44%	42%

Company A appears to be more efficient, but the figures could be affected by the different accounting treatment of certain factory costs, such as power and property costs. Company A might treat these costs as general overheads, whereas Company B might allocate them to production costs. Overall net profit would of course be unaffected.

Not realising that the figures have been manipulated

This may have been done within the rules. Consider a company that usually operates with a bank overdraft. However, the managers do not pay suppliers in the last three weeks of the trading period in order to show no bank borrowings in the balance sheet. This is unfair to suppliers but a common practice. The balance sheet will of course show trade creditors being higher than usual.

The opposite practice may also be encountered. This is paying suppliers just before the balance sheet date in order to establish a false, or at least untypical, record for paying suppliers promptly. An even more dubious practice is to draw the cheques just before the balance sheet date but not release them for some time.

Not taking account of different lengths in the trading period

Consider the following:

	10 months to 31 October 2008	14 months to 31 December 2009
Sales in period	£6,000,000	£8,400,000
Net profit before tax	£720,000	£1,008,000

Although the second period seems better, if you allow for the different lengths the results are identical, with the profit percentage being 12% in each case.

Not taking account of seasonal factors

This is a common mistake. Consider Mr Khan who starts selling ice cream from a van on 1 October. Information from his first two six-monthly profit statements is shown below.

	6 months to 31 March	6 months to 30 September
Sales in period	£12,400	£37,200
Net profit before tax	£4,216	£12,276
Profit as a percentage of sales	34%	33%

At first glance this shows that the second period is much better than the first, but this would not be the correct conclusion, although further investigation may show that there was some improvement. The reason for this conclusion is that the sale of ice cream from vans in Britain is heavily affected by the weather and the amount of daylight. Sales should be much higher in the summer months.

Profit to turnover

This is possibly the simplest of the ratios and one of the most commonly used. It is profit expressed as a percentage of turnover in the year. Sometimes profit after tax is used and sometimes profit before tax. Some analysts prefer to use profit before deducting interest and other financing charges. The following are all three calculations for Cotswold Components plc.

	£000	£000	£000
Turnover	36,129	36,129	36,129
Profit after tax	3,015		
Profit before tax		3,937	
Profit before interest payable			4,349
Profit to turnover	8.3%	10.9%	12.0%

This accounting ratio is often quoted by people who say *'look after the top line and the bottom line will look after itself'*. They may assert that if Cotswold Components plc had achieved an extra £1,000,000 turnover, profit after tax would have increased by £83,000. There is often an element of truth in this saying, but the relationship can be very tenuous. The extra profit may well have been more because the costs may not have increased by the equivalent percentage. On the other hand, if disproportionate expenditure was necessary to obtain the extra sales, the extra profit may have been less or non-existent.

Gross profit margin

In a manufacturing or trading business, gross profit (or gross loss) is the difference between sales and the costs of manufacturing or buying the products sold. In a service business it is the difference between sales and the direct cost of providing the service. In both cases overheads are excluded from the calculation. The following is the calculation for Cotswold Components plc:

	£000
Sales	36,129
Cost of sales	22,116
Gross profit margin	14,013
Gross profit margin as a percentage	38.8%

Gross margin is particularly important in many businesses because cost of sales is usually by far the biggest cost. If the cost of sales can be reduced by a few percentage points, it can have a big impact on net profit on the bottom line. British supermarkets are just one example of businesses that work hard, and often successfully, to hold down the cost of sales and maintain a satisfactory gross profit margin.

Interest cover

This is an important and much-studied ratio, especially when borrowing is high relative to shareholders' funds. This situation, known as being highly geared, is explained in the next section. It is also particularly significant when the interest charge is high relative to profits. Obviously a company that cannot pay its interest charge has severe problems and might not be able to carry on, at least not without a fresh injection of funds.

Interest cover is profit before interest and tax divided by the interest charge. The higher the resulting number the more easily the business is managing to pay the interest charge. The calculation for Cotswold Components plc is as follows:

	£000
Interest	412
Operating profit	4,349
Interest cover	10.6 times

Gearing

This ratio compares the finance provided by banks and other lenders with the capital provided by the owners. It is much used by banks who might not like to see a ratio of 1 to 1 (or some other such proportion) exceeded. It is sometimes expressed as a proportion, as in 1 to 1, and sometimes as a percentage. The calculation for Cotswold Components plc is as follows:

	£000
Loans	4,300
Shareholders' funds	5,968
Gearing	0.7 to 1

A company is said to be lowly geared when borrowing is low in relation to shareholders' funds, and this indicates a secure, safe position. An adventurous, though perhaps foolish, person might say that it indicates a boring position. A consequence is that a change in profits, up or down, will have less effect on return on capital employed than if the company had been highly geared. On the other hand, a company is highly geared when borrowing is high in relation to shareholders' funds, and this indicates a position that is less secure and less safe. A consequence is that a change in profits, up or down, will have a big effect on return on capital employed. The following figures illustrate this:

	Company A	Company B
Loans (in £000s)	40,000	160,000
Shareholders' funds (in £000s)	160,000	40,000
Gearing	1 to 4	4 to 1
Profit after tax (in £000s)	16,000	4,000
Return on capital employed	10.0%	10.0%

Both companies are achieving a return on capital of 10% but Company B is much more highly geared. Now look at what happens if both companies increase their profits by £3 million:

	Company A	Company B
Loans (in £000s)	40,000	160,000
Shareholders' funds (in £000s)	160,000	40,000
Gearing	1 to 4	4 to 1
Profit after tax (in £000s)	19,000	7,000
Return on capital employed	11.9%	17.5%

Your reaction may be that it is better to be highly geared. This may well be true if the business is secure and highly profitable, but look what happens if profits drop by £3 million:

	Company A	Company B
Loans (in £000s)	40,000	160,000
Shareholders' funds (in £000s)	160,000	40,000
Gearing	1 to 4	4 to 1
Profit after tax (in £000s)	13,000	1,000
Return on capital employed	8.1%	2.5%

There are of course many ways of looking at the figures and it is up to you to draw sensible conclusions in individual circumstances. It is certainly true that many spectacularly successful businesses have been highly geared, but it is also true that many spectacular collapses have occurred in similar circumstances.

Liquidity

Companies are not forced into involuntary liquidation because they are not making profits, although this is, of course, extremely unhelpful. It is, perhaps surprisingly, not uncommon for companies to go into liquidation that are trading profitably at the time. This is particularly true of companies that have expanded rapidly. The immediate cause of business failure is usually that they run out of liquid resources and cannot pay their debts as they become due. A balance sheet will reveal vital information about working capital and liquid resources, and it is possible that impending problems may be predicted.

A balance sheet should (and a published balance sheet must) separate assets capable of being turned into cash quickly from assets held for the long term. The former are called current assets.

Similarly, a balance sheet should separate liabilities payable in the short term – current liabilities – from those payable in the long term. The dividing point is usually one year.

The difference between current assets and current liabilities is the working capital. This is sometimes called net current assets, or net current liabilities if the liabilities are greater. The position for Cotswold Components plc is as follows:

	£000
Current assets	8,906
Less current liabilities	6,715
	2,191

Another frequently used ratio is the so-called quick ratio or acid test. This is more demanding than the working capital calculation because, of the current assets, only debtors, investments, bank and cash are used, and the total of these is compared with the total of current liabilities. Only the most liquid of the current assets are brought into the calculation. Stock is excluded because it almost always takes longer to turn into cash than debtors. If stock is excluded, the position for Cotswold Components plc is as follows:

	£000
Applicable current assets	6,790
Less total current liabilities	6,715
	75

Stock turn

This is the number of times that total stock is used (turned over) in the course of a year. There is scope for misunderstanding and it is normally applied to all stock, rather than just to finished stock. The calculation for Cotswold Components plc is as follows:

	£000
Cost of sales for year	22,116
Stock at balance sheet date	2,116
Stock turn	10.5 times

Put another way, stock was held for an average of 35 days. The calculation is:

$$\frac{365}{10.5} = 35 \text{ days}$$

Cost of sales should be obtainable from the profit and loss account, and stock should be obtainable from the balance sheet. However, a word of caution is necessary. The balance sheet gives the stock figure at a single date and that date may not be typical of the profit and loss period, especially if the company is expanding or contracting or if the business is seasonal. A more reliable figure for stock turn might be obtained if the average of several stock figures during the period is used, though in practice this might be difficult to obtain. Fortunately, published accounts must give comparable figures for the previous period and balance sheet date.

It is usually reasonable to conclude that the higher the stock turn the better, and a high stock turn is an indication that a business is being efficiently run. Some years ago certain Japanese companies became famous for their 'just in time' ordering systems, and a few even managed to maintain stock levels measured in production hours, rather than days, weeks or months. The rest of the world has been catching up and British supermarkets are examples of businesses that are very efficient in this respect, though some suppliers have been known to complain that the success has been obtained at their expense.

Despite all the advantages of a high stock turn the theory should not be tested to destruction. It is not efficient to run out of stock, have to suspend production or leave customers staring at empty shelves. It may be wise to keep higher stocks of key components or the most popular items for sale. It may also be wise to keep higher stocks if the sources of supply are insecure or not responsive to an increase in demand. A company vulnerable to industrial disputes at its suppliers is an example.

Return on capital employed

This is often abbreviated to ROCE and sometimes given the alternative name of 'Return on investment' or ROI. It is profit expressed as a percentage of the net value of the money invested in the business. Many people believe that it is the most important of the accounting ratios.

Capital employed is the balance sheet total, which in the case of a company is share capital plus reserves. This is 'shareholders' funds', which is the same as assets less liabilities. Sometimes profit before tax is used and sometimes profit after tax is used. Exceptional items may be included or excluded and so may interest. Profit after interest and after tax is the most commonly used figure.

The calculation for Cotswold Components plc, using profit after tax, is as follows:

	£000
Profit after tax	3,015
Capital employed	5,968
Return on capital employed	50.5%

In most cases this would be considered very good.

Normally, the profit for the year is compared with capital employed, as shown in the balance sheet at the end of the year. However, it is better (though in practice perhaps unnecessary) to use the average capital employed throughout the year. To obtain this you will need at least the opening and closing balance sheets.

There are two ways to improve the return on capital employed. The obvious one is to improve the profit, but an alternative is to reduce the capital employed. This can be illustrated by showing the two ways that Cotswold Components plc might have achieved a return on capital employed of 60%:

Method 1 – by increasing the profit

	£000
Profit after tax	3,581
Capital employed	5,968
Return on capital employed	60%

Method 2 – by reducing the capital employed

	£000
Profit after tax	3,015
Capital employed	5,025
Return on capital employed	60%

It may have been easier to reduce the capital employed by £943,000 than to increase the profit by £566,000.

Dividend cover

This compares the annual dividend to equity shareholders with profit after tax. It is important because it helps indicate whether or not a company has a problem paying its dividend, and whether or not the dividend may be increased, maintained or reduced in the future. The dividend cover for Cotswold Components plc is as follows:

	£000
Profit attributable to shareholders	3,015
Dividends on equity shares	920
Dividend cover	3.3 times

Dividend yield

This is the dividend per share expressed as a percentage of the current share price. The calculation for Cotswold Components plc is as follows:

Dividend per share is $\frac{920}{10,000} \times £1.00 = 9.2$ pence

Current share price is £1.64

Dividend yield is $\frac{9.2}{164} =$ 5.6%

Earnings per share

This is the net profit after tax divided by the number of issued shares. The calculation for Cotswold Components plc is as follows:

Net profit after tax	£3,015,000
Number of shares issued	10,000,000
Earnings per share	30.15 pence

Price earnings ratio

This is one of the most helpful of the investment ratios and it can be used to compare different companies in different sectors. It is often utilised to make a judgement about whether a particular company's shares are relatively cheap or relatively expensive. The higher the number, the more expensive the shares. It is often useful to do the calculation based on anticipated future earnings rather than declared historic earnings. Of course you cannot always, or indeed ever, be certain what future earnings will be.

The calculation is quoted price per share divided by earnings per share. The calculation for Cotswold Components plc is as follows:

Current share price	£1.64
Earnings per share	30.15 pence
Price earnings ratio	$\frac{164}{30.15} = 5.4$

This seems an extremely low ratio for such a profitable company, so perhaps the shares are worth buying, but, on the other hand, perhaps there are good reasons for the unfavourable rating. The profit and loss account and balance sheet reflect past performance. Perhaps the up-to-date figures are very different.

Number of days' credit given

This is the average period of credit taken by customers in paying their bills. The calculation for Cotswold Components plc is as follows:

	£000
Turnover	36,129
Trade debtors	6,724
Number of days' credit	67.9 days

The calculation is: $\dfrac{6,724 \times 365}{36,129} = 67.9$ days

Two problems should be kept in mind:

1. The turnover for a year is compared with trade debtors at a fixed date. If the figure for trade debtors is not typical of the year as a whole, the result may be misleading.
2. Turnover will probably exclude VAT, whereas the trade debtors figure will, if it is applicable, include it. At the time of writing the standard VAT rate in the UK is 17.5%. If, in the above example, all the trade debtors included 17.5% VAT, the rounded real figure for the purposes of the calculation would be £5,723,000 and the revised calculation would be:

$\dfrac{5,723 \times 365}{36,129} = 57.8$ days

Number of days' credit taken

This is, of course, the mirror image of the number of days credit given. However, you will only be able to do the calculation if you have extra information beyond that disclosed in the published accounts. This is because the figure for purchases will not be given in the profit and loss account. The figure for total costs will include such things as salaries and depreciation. The following example (not taken from Cotswold Components) assumes that it has been possible to ascertain the figure for annual purchases:

	£000
Annual purchases	64,717
Trade creditors	9,245
Number of days' credit	52.1 days

The calculation is: $\dfrac{9,245 \times 365}{64,717} = 52.1$ days

Questions to test your understanding

Given below are a company's profit and loss account for the year to 31 December, and its balance sheet at 31 December. The accounts are not in a form suitable for publication. Calculate the following:

- Profit to turnover ratio (use profit after tax).
- Gross profit margin.
- Interest cover.
- Gearing.
- Liquidity.
- Stock turn.
- Return on capital employed.
- Dividend cover.
- Dividend yield.
- Earnings per share.
- Price earnings ratio.
- Number of days' credit given (ignore possible VAT complication).

Profit Statement for the year to 31 December

	£000
Turnover	42,618
Cost of sales	29,146
Gross profit	13,472
Net operating expenses	10,006
Operating profit	3,466
Interest payable	1,904
Profit before tax	1,562
Tax	370
Profit after tax	1,192
Dividends	600
Retained profit for year	592

Balance Sheet at 31 December

	£000	£000
Fixed assets		2,106
Current assets		
Stock	2,704	
Trade debtors	6,618	
Investments	2,000	
	11,322	
Current liabilities		
Trade creditors	2,621	
Bank	6,403	
	9,024	
Net current assets		2,298
		4,404
Capital and reserves		
Called up share capital		2,500
Profit and loss account		1,904
		4,404

Other information

1. The company has issued 2,500,000 ordinary shares of £1 each.
2. The current share price is £7.76.

INSTANT TIP

If an accounting ratio seems odd or unusual, do not stop there. Look for an explanation.

Appendix A

List of International Accounting Standards in force (as at July 2008)

IFRS1	First-time adoption of international financial reporting standards
IFRS2	Share-based payment
IFRS3	Business combinations
IFRS4	Insurance contracts
IFRS5	Non-current assets held for sale and discontinued operations
IFRS6	Exploration and production assets for energy and utilities
IFRS7	Financial instruments: disclosures
IAS1	Presentation of financial statements
IAS2	Inventories
IAS7	Cash flow statements
IAS8	Accounting policies, changes in accounting estimates and errors
IAS10	Events after the balance sheet date
IAS11	Construction contracts
IAS12	Income taxes
IAS14	Segment reporting

IAS16	Property, plant and equipment
IAS17	Leases
IAS18	Revenue
IAS19	Employee benefits
IAS20	Accounting for government grants and disclosure of government assistance
IAS21	The effect of changes in foreign exchange rates
IAS23	Borrowing costs
IAS24	Related party disclosures
IAS26	Accounting and reporting by retirement benefit plans
IAS27	Consolidated and separate financial statements
IAS28	Investments in associates
IAS29	Financial reporting in hyperinflationary economies
IAS30	Disclosures in the financial statements of banks and similar financial institutions
IAS31	Interests in joint ventures
IAS32	Financial instruments: disclosure and presentation
IAS33	Earnings per share
IAS34	Interim financial reporting
IAS36	Impairment of assets
IAS37	Provisions, contingent liabilities and contingent assets
IAS38	Intangible assets
IAS39	Financial instruments: recognition and measurement
IAS40	Investment property
IAS41	Agriculture

Appendix B

List of UK Accounting Standards in force (as at July 2008)

Standards issued up to 1 August 1990 are known as Statements of Standard Accounting Practice (SSAP). Standards issued after 1 August 1990 are known as Financial Reporting Standards (FRS). Accounting standards currently in force are:

SSAP4 (Revised) The accounting treatment of government grants

SSAP5 Accounting for value added tax

SSAP9 (Revised) Stocks and long-term contracts

SSAP13 (Revised) Accounting for research and development

SSAP17 Accounting for post-balance sheet events

SSAP19 Accounting for investment properties

SSAP20 Foreign currency translation

SSAP21 Accounting for leases and hire purchase contracts

SSAP25 Segmental reporting

FRSSE Financial Reporting Standard for Smaller Entities

FRS1 (Revised)	Cash flow statements
FRS2	Accounting for subsidiary undertakings
FRS3	Reporting financial performance
FRS4	Capital instruments
FRS5	Reporting the substance of transactions
FRS6	Acquisitions and mergers
FRS7	Fair values in acquisition accounting
FRS8	Related party disclosures
FRS9	Associates and joint ventures
FRS10	Goodwill and intangible assets
FRS11	Impairment of fixed assets and goodwill
FRS12	Provisions, contingent liabilities and contingent assets
FRS13	Derivatives and other financial instruments: disclosures
FRS14	Earnings per share
FRS15	Tangible fixed assets
FRS16	Current taxation
FRS17	Retirement benefits
FRS18	Accounting policies
FRS19	Deferred tax
FRS20	Share-based payment
FRS21	Events after the balance sheet date
FRS22	Earnings per share
FRS23	The effects of changes in foreign exchange rates
FRS24	Financial reporting in hyperinflationary economies
FRS25	Financial Instruments: Disclosure and Presentation
FRS26	Financial Instruments: Measurement
FRS27	Life Assurance
FRS28	Corresponding amounts
FRS29	Financial instruments: disclosures

Answers to questions asked in this book

Chapter 1

1. Credit gives the benefit.
2. The entries are as follows:

Subscriptions

Debit	£		Credit	£
		Bank Account		200

Bank Account

Debit	£		Credit	£
Subscriptions	200	Rent		500
Donations received	5,000			

Rent

Debit	£		Credit	£
Bank Account	500			

Legal and Professional

Debit	£		Credit	£
Lafferty and Reed	300			

K. Klaus Ltd

Debit	£		Credit	£
		Printing		170

Printing

Debit	£		Credit	£
K. Klaus Ltd.	170			

Donations Received

Debit	£		Credit	£
		Bank Account		5,000

Lafferty and Reed

Debit	£		Credit	£
		Legal and Professional		300

Chapter 2

1.

Plant and machinery	asset	debit balance	balance sheet
Sales	income	credit balance	profit and loss account
Wages	expenditure	debit balance	profit and loss account
Capital reserves	capital	credit balance	balance sheet
Cash	asset	debit balance	balance sheet
Telephone	expenditure	debit balance	profit and loss account
Computer equipment	asset	debit balance	balance sheet
Bank account (with an overdraft)	liability	credit balance	balance sheet
Six Per Cent Preference shares	capital	credit balance	balance sheet
Rent	expenditure	debit balance	profit and loss account

2. The sales ledger control account is a single account in the nominal ledger. The total of all the balances in the sales ledger add to the balance of the sales ledger control account. Any change to a sales ledger account affects the balance of it. The balance of the sales ledger control account is the total amount owing to the business by all the customers.

3. No.

4.

		Debit £	Credit £
4 June	Sales ledger control account		777
JV 71	Bad debts written off	777	

To write off as irrecoverable balance owing by F. Smith Ltd.

		Debit £	Credit £
4 June	Bad debt reserve account		6,000
JV 72	Bad debts written off	6,000	

To create a general bad debt reserve

Chapter 3

1. Yes – because each entry should be ticked individually

2.

Cash book balance at 30 June		1,856.08 dr
Add payments in cash book not on statement		
316	77.22	
319	16.12	
320	17.81	
321	44.44	
		155.59
		2,011.67
Less receipt in cash book		
not on statement		720.66
		1,291.01
Less payment on statement		
not in cash book		117.48
As per statement balance at 30 June		1,173.53 dr

Chapter 4

1.

Stock Account

Debit		£	Credit		£
1 July	Balance b/f	99,000	12 July	Profit and Loss Account	3,000
4 July	Cash Account	14,000			
6 July	Knight Ltd	8,000	17 July	Profit and Loss Account	121,900
8 July	Knight Ltd	6,000			

Cash Account

Debit		£	Credit		£
12 July	Sales	4,200	4 July	Stock Account	14,000

Knight Ltd

Debit		£	Credit		£
16 July	Stock Account	2,100	6 July	Stock Account	8,000
			8 July	Stock Account	6,000

Returns Outwards Account

Debit	£	Credit		£
		16 July	Knight Ltd	2,100

Profit and Loss Account

Debit		£	Credit	£
12 July	Stock Account	3,000		
17 July	Stock Account	121,900		

Sales

Debit			Credit
	£		£
		12 July Cash account	4,200

2.   Yes.

3.

Stock Account

Debit		Credit
	£	£
3 May	10,000	

VAT Account

Debit		Credit
	£	£
3 May	1,750	

Claphorn and Crayfish Ltd

Debit		Credit
	£	£
	3 May	11,750

4.

	Debit	Credit
	£	£
Bank Account		61,216.13
Wages Suspense Account	61,216.13	
Wages Suspense Account		61,216.13
PAYE Owing Account		15,123.45
Employees' National Insurance Account		9,678.32
Employer's National Insurance Account		10,996.42
Staff Loan Account		500.00
Production Department Salaries Account	63,111.48	
Administration Department Salaries Account	34,402.84	
	158,730.45	158,730.45

5. The three types of error that will not be disclosed by a trial balance are:

- A compensating error.
- An error of principle.
- A transaction omitted altogether

Chapter 5

1. The sales ledger control account would be unlikely to agree to the total of the individual sales ledger accounts following this journal, and a good computerised bookkeeping package would highlight this before the entry is successfully posted. Likewise, the VAT control account might not agree to the VAT return following the posting of the journal.
2. (a) 0, (b) 2, (c) 1, (d) 5, (e) 6.
3. 'S' indicates standard-rated (currently 17.5%) and the VAT would be £525.
4. (c) is not currently possible – changes in the tax law would need to be entered manually into a spreadsheet. (a) is possible using the ROUND function; (b) is achieved using Tools/Formula Auditing/Trace Dependents, and (d) is calculated by entering two dates and subtracting one from the other, ensuring that the resultant cell is in number format rather than date format.

Chapter 6

1. Straight line method

	£
Cost	16,000
Year 1 25% × £16,000	4,000
	12,000
Year 2 25% × £16,000	4,000
Written-down value at end of year 2	8,000

Reducing balance method

Cost	16,000
Year 1 25% × £16,000	4,000
	12,000
Year 2 25% × £12,000	3,000
Written-down value at end of year 2	9,000

2.

	Debit	Credit
	£	£
Prepayments account	70	
Food purchased account		70
Accruals account		400
Telephone account	400	
Prepayments account	600	
Water rates account		600
Accruals account		700
Food purchased account	700	
Accruals account		250
Wages account	250	

3. Journal for first year

	Debit £	Credit £
Provision for discounts deducted		15,000
Sales	15,000	

To set up provision of 2.5% of
total amount owing by customers.

Journal for following year

	Debit £	Credit £
Provision for discounts deducted	15,000	
Sales		15,000

To reverse provision made at
end of previous year.

Note: Discount actually deducted by customers will be debited to sales as the payments are received. The net effect of the £8,000 of debits and the £15,000 journal credit will be an increase in profit of £7,000 in the following year.

Chapter 7

1.

Bernard Smith
Profit and Loss Account for year to 31 May

	£	£
Invoiced sales		15,000
Less Costs:		
Materials used	2,000	
Motor expenses	1,400	
Other overhead costs	3,700	
Depreciation	1,600	
Bad debt	350	
Remedial work	200	
		9,250
Net profit		5,750

2.

North West Novelties Ltd
Profit and Loss Account for year to 30 April

	£	£
Sales		600,000
Opening stock	50,000	
Add purchases	200,000	
	250,000	
Less closing stock	40,000	
	210,000	
Production wages	280,000	
Other production costs	90,000	
Cost of manufacturing		580,000
		20,000
Less total overheads		60,000
Net loss for year		(40,000)

Chapter 8

1. No! It lists the assets and liabilities as at a fixed point in time.
2. £30,000.

3.

Peter Harvey

Profit and Loss Account for the year to 31 March

	£	£
Sales		28,776
Less expenses:		
Bad debts written off	240	
Charitable donations	200	
Depreciation	2,500	
Electricity	270	
Insurance	590	
Office expenses	1,660	
Postage	168	
Rent	2,000	
Telephone	413	
Travel expenses	3,988	
		12,029
Net profit		16,747

Peter Harvey
Balance Sheet as at 31 March

	£	£
Fixed assets		
Motor vehicle		5,000
Current assets		
Bank	22,198	
Trade debtors	842	
	23,040	
Less current liabilities		
Trade creditors	661	
Net current assets		22,379
		27,379
Capital employed		
At beginning of period	10,632	
Add profit for year	16,747	
		27,379

Chapter 9

1. Yes it is, but the accounts delivered to Companies House may omit certain information in the accounts sent to the members.
2. The accounts must give a 'true and fair view'.
3. No – the profit and loss account must be set out in the way required by the law and accounting standards. These do not permit profit after tax to be put at the top.
4. No – debts due up to one year must be shown separately.
5. Yes.
6. Only if it is a quoted company.
7. Nine months from the accounting reference date.

Chapter 10

Profit to turnover ratio

	£000
Turnover	42,618
Profit after tax	1,192
Profit to turnover	2.8%

Gross profit margin

	£000
Sales	42,618
Cost of sales	29,146
Gross profit margin	13,472
Gross profit margin as a percentage	31.6%

Interest cover

	£000
Interest	1,904
Operating profit	3,466
Interest cover	1.8 times

Gearing

	£000
Loans	6,403
Shareholders' funds	4,404
Gearing	1.5 to 1

Liquidity

	£000
Current assets	11,322
Less current liabilities	9,024
	2,298

Stock turn

	£000
Cost of sales for year	29,146
Stock at balance sheet date	2,704
Stock turn	10.8 times

Return on capital employed

	£000
Profit after tax	1,192
Capital employed	4,404
Return on capital employed	27.1%

Dividend cover

	£000
Profit attributable to shareholders	1,192
Dividends on equity shares	600
Dividend cover	2.0 times

Dividend yield

Dividend per share is $\dfrac{600}{2,500} \times £1.00 = 24.0$ pence

Current share price is £7.76

Dividend yield is $\dfrac{24}{776} = 3.1\%$

Earnings per share

Net profit after tax	£1,192,000
Number of shares issued	2,500,000
Earnings per share	47.7 pence

Price earnings ratio

Current share price	£7.76
Earnings per share	47.7 pence
Price earnings ratio	16.3

Number of days credit given

	£000
Turnover	42,618
Trade debtors	6,618
Number of days' credit	56.7 days

The calculation is: $\dfrac{6,618 \times 365}{42,618}$ = 56.7 days

Further reading

Accounting for Non-Accounting Students, John Dyson (Pearson Education, 2007)

Basic Accounting, J. Randall Scott and Mike Truman (*Teach Yourself* series, Hodder Education, 2003)

Bookkeeping, A. G. Piper and Andrew Lymer (*Teach Yourself* series, Hodder Education, 2006)

Book-Keeping and Accounts, Frank Wood and Sheila Robinson (Pearson Education, 2004)

Bookkeeping for Dummies, Lita Epstein (John Wiley and Sons, 2005)

Bookkeeping Made Easy, Roy Hedges (Lawpack Publishing)

Business Plans, David Lloyd (*Instant Manager* series, Hodder Education, 2007)

Cash Flow for Small Businesses, Robert McCallion and Alan Warner (*Teach Yourself* series, Hodder Education, 2008)

Excel 2007, Moira Stephen (*Teach Yourself* series, Hodder Education, 2007)

Finance for Non-Financial Managers, Roger Mason (*Instant Manager* series, Hodder Education, 2007)

Financial Accounting, Augustine Benedict and Barry Elliott (Pearson Education, 2008)

Mastering Book-Keeping, Peter Marshall (How to Books, 2007)

PowerPoint 2007, Moira Stephen (*Teach Yourself* series, Hodder Education, 2007)

Sage Line 50, Mac Bride (*Teach Yourself* series, Hodder Education, 2006)

Shaum's Outline of Principles of Accounting, Joel Lerner and James Cashin (McGraw Hill, 2001)

Small Business Accounting, Mike Truman and David Lloyd (*Teach Yourself* series, Hodder Education, 2006)

Understanding Tax for Small Businesses, Sarah Deeks (*Teach Yourself* series, Hodder Education, 2006)

Word 2007, Moira Stephen (*Teach Yourself* series, Hodder Education, 2006)

Index